Praise for *The Nonprofit Ma*

"*The Nonprofit Marketing Guide* stands far above the cr organizations what to do communications-wise, Miller's masterpiece shows them how. It should be required reading for every nonprofit communicator."

—**Nancy E. Schwartz,** publisher, GettingAttention.org, and president, Nancy Schwartz & Company

"Kivi's book delivers solid tactics and strategies, while at the same time driving home the point that nonprofit marketing should have a soul. Whatever your marketing strategy, this book is sure to challenge your ideas and present you with fantastic opportunities for the future."

—**Danielle Brigida,** social media outreach coordinator, National Wildlife Federation

"Kivi makes marketing doable for nonprofits, uses colorful examples to demonstrate her topics, and has practical and cost-effective tips for immediate implementation to improve marketing efforts."

—**Magda Hageman-Apol,** assistant vice president and director of the National Center for Nutrition Leadership, Meals On Wheels Association of America

"If I could only select one communications book for the lending library at our Nonprofit Resource Center, *The Nonprofit Marketing Guide* would be my top choice. This practical, no-nonsense guide is written in terms everyone can understand, for any mission, with any audience."

—**Susie Bowie,** communications associate, The Community Foundation of Sarasota County

"Whew! Finally there's a guide to help nonprofits with limited resources navigate the unbelievably fast-paced and ever-changing world of marketing. Thanks, Kivi!"

—**Sheri Booms Holm,** communications director, West Central Initiative

"In *The Nonprofit Marketing Guide,* Kivi Leroux Miller, a one-person marketing department veteran, has distilled the overwhelming topic of nonprofit marketing into a plan of attack. Whether you've worked in nonprofit marketing for one month or ten years, you will benefit from her practical and high-impact strategies for success."

—**Valerie Stoj,** development and PR director, Ollie Webb Center, Inc.

"Facing a world on information overload, your nonprofit may be at the cross roads . . . needing a marketing jolt to step into the world of new media and viral marketing. There is no one better than Kivi Leroux Miller to walk your team, step-by-step, into this new realm. Whether making your website sparkle or launching your first e-newsletter, Kivi understands the challenges and limitations nonprofits face and offers practical tools that are timely, cost effective, and fun."

—**Kathy Padro,** social marketing consultant for hospice and healthcare organizations

"Having had a career in marketing prior to coming to work for a nonprofit, I know that marketing can be an organization's biggest, yet most important, expense. Kivi's advice in this book will help nonprofit marketers 'think outside the box' to come up with creative, inexpensive, and effective marketing strategies. Kivi works diligently to help good causes on a shoestring budget be successful."

—**Elaine Dhuyvetter,** assistant director, Greater Manhattan Community Foundation

"This booked is filled with practical advice, tips, and checklists—everything you need in one book to help your nonprofit organization create and implement a marketing plan that gets results!"

—**Beth Kanter,** blogger, *Beth's Blog,* and coauthor, *The Networked Nonprofit*

"Brilliant and comprehensive! Kivi Leroux Miller covers all the bases in this lively and insightful guide to marketing for nonprofit organizations. The breadth of her experience on both sides of the consultant-client divide shows clearly here. If you're responsible for marketing and communications and stretched to the limit and beyond, buy this book. You'll soon see how much easier your job becomes."

—**Mal Warwick,** author, *Fundraising When Money Is Tight* and *How to Write Successful Fundraising Letters*

"*The Nonprofit Marketing Guide* provides needed direction for busy nonprofit professionals who find themselves doing multiple jobs without time to focus on effective marketing and communications. This book relieves the feeling of being overwhelmed and provides strategic direction for our valuable resources of time and money."

—**Allison Treppa,** director of marketing and communications, Michigan Nonprofit Association

"As a tiny nonprofit with a total budget of about $100,000, we obviously have very little set aside for marketing. Kivi understands our situation and provides practical, useful, low-cost marketing advice that produces great results."

—**Danielle Denhardt,** board of directors, Fancy Cats Rescue Team

The Nonprofit Marketing Guide

HIGH-IMPACT, LOW-COST WAYS TO BUILD SUPPORT FOR YOUR GOOD CAUSE

Kivi Leroux Miller

Foreword by
Katya Andresen

Published by Jossey-Bass
A Wiley Imprint
989 Market Street, San Francisco, CA 94103-1741—www.josseybass.com

Jossey-Bass books and products are available through most bookstores. To contact Jossey-Bass directly call our Customer Care Department within the U.S. at 800-956-7739, outside the U.S. at 317-572-3986, or fax 317-572-4002.

Jossey-Bass also publishes its books in a variety of electronic formats. Some content that appears in print may not be available in electronic books.

Library of Congress Cataloging-in-Publication Data
Leroux Miller, Kivi, date.
The nonprofit marketing guide : high-impact, low-cost ways to build support for your good cause / Kivi Leroux Miller ; foreword by Katya Andresen. — 1st ed.
p. cm. — (The Jossey-Bass nonprofit guidebook series ; 10)
Includes index.
ISBN 978-0-470-53965-1 (pbk.)
1. Nonprofit organizations—Marketing. I. Title.
HF5415.L474 2010
658.8—dc22

2010003894

Printed in the United States of America
FIRST EDITION
PB Printing V00261_070918

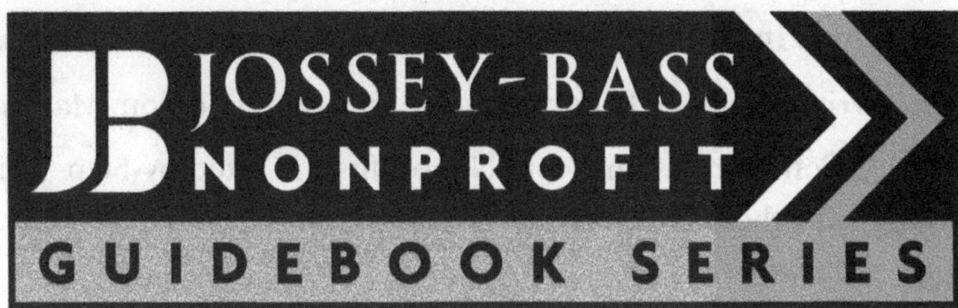

The Jossey-Bass Nonprofit Guidebook Series

The Jossey-Bass Nonprofit Guidebook Series provides new to experienced nonprofit professionals and volunteers with the essential tools and practical knowledge they need to make a difference in the world. From hands-on workbooks to step-by-step guides on developing a critical skill or learning how to perform an important task or process, our accomplished expert authors provide readers with the information required to be effective in achieving goals, mission, and impact.

Other Titles in The Jossey-Bass Nonprofit Guidebook Series

How to Write Successful Fundraising Letters, Second Edition, *Mal Warwick*

Strategic Communications for Nonprofits: A Step-by-Step Guide to Working with the Media, Second Edition, *Kathy Bonk, Emily Tynes, Henry Griggs, and Phil Sparks*

Winning Grants: Step by Step, Third Edition, *Mim Carlson, Tori O'Neal-McElrath, The Alliance for Nonprofit Management*

The Budget-Building Book for Nonprofits: A Step-by-Step Guide for Managers and Boards, Second Edition, *Murray Dropkin, Jim Halpin, and Bill La Touche*

The Executive Director's Guide to Thriving as a Nonprofit Leader, Second Edition (*formerly* The Executive Director's Survival Guide: Thriving as a Nonprofit Leader), *Mim Carlson, Margaret Donohoe*

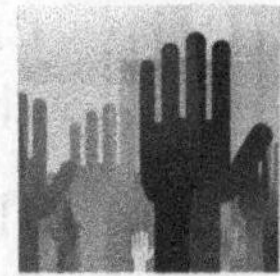

CONTENTS

FOREWORD

Katya Andresen

Thank you for picking up this book. Because it has caught your interest, you probably believe that we as nonprofit professionals need to know marketing—no matter how small, how underbudgeted, or how overworked we may be.

We need more people like you.

Why? Because we cannot afford *not* to do marketing. You cannot move people without it. As worthy as our causes may be, simply telling people that what we do matters is not an outreach strategy. It's not enough to plaster our mission statement on our home page or tell people what's good for them. We can't talk at them; we have to communicate with them. That means listening to the people we want to reach, learning from what we hear, and shaping our outreach accordingly. We need to shift from old-fashioned spray-and-pray marketing (that is, telling a lot of people something and hoping it sticks for some of them) to a respectful, two-way relationship with our supporters. They expect this of us, and they stop supporting us when they don't get that kind of attention and cultivation.

We need people who understand this throughout all levels of organizations, from executive directors to communications departments to fundraising staff. We need to infuse the culture of our nonprofits with a keen and unwavering focus on the people we serve, the individuals we're seeking to influence, and the donors we cultivate. Strong marketing and communications help us shift from a preaching to a persuasion perspective, making everything we do work better.

This is a handbook for making this happen. I wish I could tuck a team of marketers and a wad of cash for your cause into the back of the book, but the content is the next best thing. It will do two things for you. First, it will make you feel like you have a peppy, witty, and wise personal mentor in promoting your cause. Second, if you apply the principles in these pages, this book will make you a more effective and versatile marketer who can build deep and lasting relationships with supporters. You'll master how to galvanize people to action, which will translate into a bigger base, more money, and greater impact.

We need that more than ever right now. At the time of this writing, the economy is performing poorly, giving is down, and competition is up. In the United States alone, there are more than 1.8 million nonprofits, and a hundred new ones form every day. More organizations are competing for fewer resources.

Fortunately, this book recognizes these limitations without limiting your marketing potential. This book was written for nonprofits with small staff and meager resources, which describes most of us, and it shows us all how to do more with less. Through working smarter and communicating better, we *can* have great impact without deep pockets.

That's a message close to my heart. There is so much need in the world that we have no choice but to do a better job at our jobs. Our modest resources must not translate into modest impact. Too many lives and livelihoods are at stake.

I suspect you're with me on this, or you wouldn't have this book in your hands. And I am so very glad you do, because, again, the world needs more people like you—those determined to learn how to reach more people and do more good, however modest the means at their disposal.

Let me tell you a story. On my recent trip to Seoul to take part in a conference of the fledgling nonprofit sector, the director of the South Korea–based Beautiful Foundation handed me a plastic bank and a stuffed figure, both in the shape of a smiling bean. When I asked what beans had to do with philanthropy, she explained that even something as small as a bean can be divided infinitely and shared broadly. It's an apt symbol for giving, and HappyBean is the name of the Foundation's portal for donations and nonprofit blogs in Korea. It's a clever way to express the importance of being resourceful in the face of scarcity—and a great marketing package with real participation for supporters. These are the kinds of tools we need to succeed in getting people to take action.

Kivi, the author of this book, is at that level of resourcefulness, so you're in good hands. I'll never forget meeting Kivi. I'd followed her work for about a year online, marveling at her communication trainings, her blog, and her many resource guides. She was a prodigiously prolific and creative thought leader with an impressive consulting practice and a large following. I imagined she must be some kind of nonprofit marketing mogul with a full staff in slick city offices.

Then we ended up crossing paths at a nonprofit conference, and I discovered that while most of this was true, there was one big exception. Kivi had done all of this by herself, in a home office, with almost no money, powered with little more than her smart mind and her incredible desire to teach, train, and give the gift of knowledge to people doing good works. Over coffee she asked, "Should I write a book, too?" My response? Heck, yes. I couldn't imagine anyone more qualified to write about marketing on a shoestring. And a short two years later, here is her wonderful work.

In reading about the many ways you can use marketing to advance your mission, I hope you'll be energized by and awakened to the many ways it can make a difference in your work, from growing a movement, to inspiring staff, to raising money. As a professional marketer, I admit to bias, but I think virtually all of our work can being strengthened by our becoming better marketers—namely, mastering how to compel others to take the actions we want them to—as well as more effective communicators who can create and deliver the right messages in the right places at the right time. And good marketing and communications tend to make us far better fundraisers.

This is where the small nonprofit has an advantage. At enormous organizations, executive staff, marketers, communicators, and fundraisers operate in organizational silos. For the rest of us, the lines are blurred and we likely play many of these roles at once. Although it's hard to wear many hats, at least doing so makes us more integrated in our marketing, communications, and fundraising work (all of which are covered in this book). It also makes it easier to implement the many good ideas in this book.

Great changes are in reach, thanks to this guide. Good luck and Godspeed as you make them happen.

Katya Andresen is the chief operating officer of Network for Good and the author of *Robin Hood Marketing: Stealing Corporate Savvy to Sell Just Causes.*

For Edgar, Ava, and Jia,
the pot of gold at the end of my rainbow

PREFACE: WHY I WROTE THIS BOOK

When I started my consulting business in 1998, I thought I'd make a living as a freelance writer and editor for environmental organizations. Thus EcoScribe Communications was born. I had worked for the U.S. Environmental Protection Agency and for a small foundation in San Francisco, and I had served on the boards of and volunteered with numerous nonprofits. I saw plenty of need for a good writer who understood both the issues and the nonprofit world.

But within a matter of months, clients were asking me if I could not only write their newsletter, but lay it out too. And could I get bids from the printer while I was at it? And convert it to a PDF and put in on the website? Could I not only whip up a press release, but call a few reporters too?

Before long, I was updating website copy, digitally cleaning up photos, and designing web pages. I went from reviewing *The Elements of Style* to setting styles in Adobe Photoshop, PageMaker, InDesign, and Dreamweaver. I thought more about the rules of HTML and PHP than the rules of good grammar. Soon I was not only implementing tactics for clients, but also creating their marketing strategies, drafting their communications budgets, and attempting to calculate return-on-investment for all of this work.

Some fellow freelance writers who struck out on their own at the same time were floundering, while my business was flourishing. Why? Because I had quickly realized that the staff at nonprofits who were assigned the communications and marketing work were completely overwhelmed. The writing was only one small piece of the job—they needed so much more done than a writer alone could provide.

Good marketing requires a complex set of skills, yet the small nonprofits who hired me had neither those skills on staff nor the budgets to hire multiple consultants. For a few clients, I became their entire communications department. I had to either do it myself or, in a few cases, find very reasonably priced subcontractors to help me out, or the work wouldn't get done. It certainly wasn't a perfect solution for me or for my nonprofit clients, but we made it work, because it was the only option.

Over the following decade, I learned how to be that nonprofit marketing department of one. I experimented all the time, producing both successes and failures, but always learning. I spent more money that I care to admit on software, handbooks, and training courses to learn all I thought I needed to know—some of which was priceless, some of which was a complete waste of time and hard-earned cash. But the one book I really could have used, the one that would have saved me immense amounts of time, money, and frustration, didn't exist. I vowed that at some point later in life I would write it myself.

All the while, I had been teaching workshops, first through the Social Action and Leadership School for Activists (SALSA) program in Washington, D.C., and then through Duke University's certificate program in nonprofit management. Because I enjoyed teaching so much, in 2007 I decided to transition my business from primarily consulting to primarily training. I launched NonprofitMarketingGuide.com, including a blog and weekly webinar series. My hunch that staff at thousands of nonprofits were in the exact same situation that my clients and I had been in for many years was right: they too were communications departments of just one or two people who had to do it all themselves and didn't know where to turn for help.

Since then, hardly a week passed in which I didn't receive a note of gratitude from an overwhelmed executive director, development director, or communications manager. They were so relieved to find the resources, tips, and guidance I'm creating and compiling from others, which they so desperately need to do their jobs well for their good causes. I knew that the time to write this book had arrived.

I've tried to share the best of what I've learned over the last decade. I had to make some difficult decisions about what to focus on and what to leave out (for example, you'll find only a small amount of branding, advertising, and graphic design advice in this book).

I'm still learning every day and sharing what I learn at nonprofitmarketing guide.com. We've created a special section on the site especially for book buyers like you: www.nonprofitmarketingguide.com/book. You'll find more information on accessing those resources at the end of the book—so that when you're through reading, we can continue the conversation, the learning, and the sharing there.

Kivi Leroux Miller
April 2010

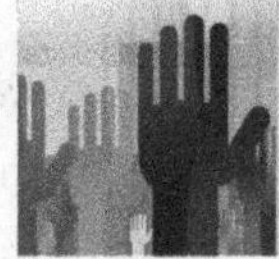

ACKNOWLEDGMENTS

First, I want to thank all of the people this book is for and about, at thousands of small nonprofits across North America and the world. Since I launched nonprofitmarketingguide.com in late 2007 and the weekly webinar series in 2008, you have inspired me every day to do whatever I can to help you in your quest to create a better world. Special thanks to all of the site's biggest fans, including Judy Anderson, Tara Collins, Danielle Denhardt, Elaine Dhuyvetter, Amy Falken, Amy Good, Sheri Holm, Fran Simon, Valerie Stoj, and Andrea Umbreit.

I'm especially grateful to the following nonprofit leaders who shared the stories that appear in the book: John Bell, Amy Cherry, Leslie Collins, Ceci Dadisman, Mark Ferguson, Beth Krusi, Marta Lindsey, Lane Phalen, Stephanie Sides, Kelly Stettner, Cari Turley, Ari Wallach, Gordon Wright, and David Zermeno.

A robust, thought-provoking, inspiring, and funny cadre of bloggers who write about nonprofit marketing, fundraising, and technology have influenced my thinking and approaches to many topics in this book. Kudos to Jeff Brooks, Sarah Durham, Allison Fine, Jocelyn Harmon, John Haydon, Beth Kanter, Rebecca Leaman, Gordon Mayer, Gail Perry, Gayle Thorsen, and Nedra Weinreich for your always helpful insights.

Three additional bloggers deserve special recognition, because they have become not only cheerleaders for my business and this book, but also dear friends.

Katya Andresen made my dream of writing this book come true. The first time we met in person, Katya offered to review my book outline and later introduced me to her editor—now also mine—Jesse Wiley, and to her agent—again, now also mine—Mollie Glick. You wouldn't be holding this finished book right now were it not for her generous spirit. Be sure to read her inspiring foreword.

Nancy Schwartz keeps me thinking long, laughing hard, and dreaming big. What better blogging buddy could a girl ask for? She's an excellent conference roomie as well.

Claire Meyerhoff is the creative yin to my pragmatic yang. Together we produce Magic Keys Radio and Podcast. She makes nonprofit marketing more fun than I thought possible (and I already thought it was pretty fun).

Jesse Wiley has been a wonderful, supportive, and flexible advocate for this book within Jossey-Bass from day one. Joanne Fritz, Janet Gluch, Vince Hyman, Sandra Sims, and Allison Treppa provided over fifty pages of notes on my first draft. I can honestly say that reviewing their feedback and using it to improve the book was one of the most positive experiences of my writing career. Vince's words of wisdom were especially helpful to me in resolving several conflicts within my own head. Thanks also to the entire team at Jossey-Bass for improving the book at every step along the way between my desk and yours.

My dear friend Rebecca Jamison, who finished her first book years before I did, inspired me to pick up the pace on mine and invited me along for a very productive writing retreat in Niagara-on-the-Lake six weeks before my first draft was due, when I was still floundering about. It was a genuine turning point in the life of this book.

My aunt Robin Holloway, grandma Jackie Holloway, and my parents, Bob and Sue Leroux, have supported me in every decision I've made for as long as I can remember, the good and the bad. My sister and virtual assistant, Kristina Leroux Brown, helped keep my business running at full steam while I wrote the book, and she proofread the first draft for me on a ridiculous deadline.

Since July 1, 1998—the day I left California, moved into my husband Edgar's house in Washington, D.C., and started EcoScribe Communications—he has been willing to hold on tight while I fly by the seat of my pants. His great love, loyalty, and culinary skills keep me going every single day. He's also the best dad in the world to our two young daughters: Jianna, who is my heart, and Avalon, who is my soul.

My gratitude and love to you all.

THE AUTHOR

Kivi Leroux Miller is president of EcoScribe Communications and nonprofitmarketingguide.com. Through training, coaching, and consulting, she helps small nonprofits and communications departments of one make a big impression with smart, savvy marketing and communications. She is a nationally recognized speaker who teaches a weekly webinar series and writes a leading blog on nonprofit communications.

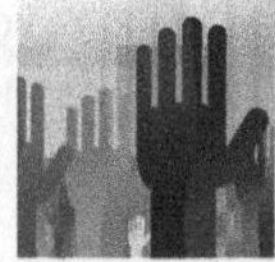

INTRODUCTION: HOW TO USE THIS BOOK

This book is meant to be part real-world survival guide and part nitty-gritty how-to handbook for busy nonprofit marketers with small budgets and staff, including executive directors who are asked to do it all. I hope it is both a reference that you'll return to often and a comforting support, reassuring you that you really can do this, even if you are working on your own. Crease up the spine, mark up the pages, and make it your own personal guide to marketing your good cause.

The book is organized into four sections.

Part One: Getting Ready to Do It Right gives you some perspective on the nonprofit marketing world today. Chapter One describes ten realities that you'll be contending with as you try to build support for your good cause. Chapter Two reviews what your nonprofit marketing plan should include in theory and what it's more likely to look like in the real world. Chapter Three explains the value of listening intently to what's being said about your nonprofit and your cause and how to set up your listening network.

Part Two: Writing a Quick-and-Dirty Marketing Plan for a Specific Program shows you how answering three deceptively simple questions can result in a marketing plan that works. Chapter Four asks, "Who do you want to reach?" and shows you how to define your target audience. Chapter Five asks, "What do you want to say?" and describes how to create a powerful message. Chapter Six asks, "How and where are you going to say it?" and reviews ways to deliver your message to your audience. Chapter Seven explains how to tell great stories about your work, which will spread your message even further.

Part Three: Building a Community of Supporters Around You recognizes the profound shift in how people and nonprofits are connecting with and relating to each other, especially online. Chapter Eight discusses ways to make it easy for new supporters to find and connect with your organization, offline and online. Chapter Nine explains how to become an expert source that the media and others will turn to. Chapter Ten looks at ways to stay in touch with your supporters regularly and frequently. Chapter Eleven explains why the simple act of sharing your gratitude with your supporters is one of the most powerful marketing tactics ever. Chapter Twelve looks at ways to empower your fans to build even more support for you.

Part Four: Doing It Yourself Without Doing Yourself In looks at the trio of elements required for successful implementation of any marketing program: time, talent, and treasure. Chapter Thirteen looks at ways to get more done in less time. Chapter Fourteen focuses on ways to improve your own marketing skills and to recruit others to help you implement your strategy. Chapter Fifteen reveals how to market your organization on a tight (or nonexistent) budget.

The book concludes with some suggestions for the big questions to ask yourself as you evaluate the success of your nonprofit marketing program.

You can approach the book in the way that works best for you: read it straight through, or backward, or start in the middle. The detailed table of contents in the front, as well as an index in the back, can help you quickly find the sections you need.

THE COMPANION WEBSITE

This book emphasizes many online strategies, not because they are new or hot, but because they are often the most affordable and fastest way for you to communicate with others. But online services change quickly. Therefore, with the exception of major names like Google and Facebook, many of my recommendations on specific tools can be found on the companion website instead, along with many more tips and how-tos. You'll find additional information on accessing the site at the back of this book.

PART ONE Getting Ready to Do It Right

Nonprofit marketing is hard work. It's also tremendously fun and satisfying, especially when you do it right. Your work will challenge you in ways you have yet to understand, and you'll learn about disciplines that you had never considered before. Because nonprofit marketing is complex, it can quickly overwhelm people new to the field. This is particularly true if it's something thrown on top of your "real" job as an executive director, development director, or program manager. This book should make your job a little easier.

In Chapter One, I review ten realities of the world today that you should incorporate into your thinking. Chapter Two gives you an overview of what a full-blown marketing strategy looks like and compares that to the quick-and-dirty plans you are more likely to produce for your specific programs and campaigns. Chapter Three explains why listening (call it market research if you prefer) is essential to any successful nonprofit marketing strategy and how you can use both offline and online tools to learn a great deal about the people you are working with and serving.

chapter
ONE

Ten New Realities for Nonprofits

Be bold and mighty forces will come to your aid.

—Basil King, author and pastor

This chapter is about . . .

- What nonprofit marketing is and isn't
- The impact of shifting demographics and the Internet on nonprofit marketing
- How the role of a nonprofit communicator is changing
- Understanding nonprofit marketing in 2010 and beyond

Many forces beyond your control affect how you market your nonprofit organization. The economy is up; the economy is down. Friendly lawmakers are in charge; then they lose the next election. Talented volunteers, staff, and board members come and go. What people can do online, and what they expect to find and do on your website, is constantly expanding. These changes have profound effects on how you communicate with your supporters.

To get the most use out of this book and to understand the choices I suggest you make, you should understand the assumptions behind it. Thus, here are ten nonprofit marketing realities I believe are now self-evident.

REALITY 1: MARKETING IS NOT A DIRTY WORD—NOR IS COMMUNICATIONS OR PUBLIC RELATIONS

In a blog post titled "Is Marketing Slimy?" Katya Andresen says, "Asking people what they care about and then relating our cause to their values is respectful. Good marketing is a conversation."

Marketing gets a bad rap because when it's done poorly, it can be downright offensive. No one wants to feel like someone, especially a charity, is trying to trick or cheat them. No one likes being yelled at, patronized, or coerced.

So don't think of your marketing program as a megaphone or a soap box. Think of it as a conversation around the dinner table or on a long walk. It's true that some communications tactics are naturally more one-way or impersonal than others, so not everything you do will have conversational elements. But your marketing program as a whole should include many opportunities for the back-and-forth dialogue with your supporters over time. You should listen and talk and listen again and respond. That's conversation. Be genuine, generous, and grateful in your conversations, and you won't slip into the slime.

It's also time for us to cast marketing in a completely different way. Now, it's often seen by budget-crunched nonprofits as an optional, feel-good task that's not central to the core mission of the organization. In reality, that couldn't be further from the truth. When you do marketing right, it helps you achieve your core mission in more powerful, effective, and efficient ways. Good marketing is as much about listening as it is about talking, and what you'll hear when you listen intently can be used to make profound, substantive changes in the way you manage all aspects of your organization, programmatic or otherwise. The content of good marketing communications is not fluff or pabulum, but meaningful substance that matters to you and your supporters.

I'm all for coming up with a better term to describe what it is I'm talking about in this book, if you think "marketing" just doesn't cut it. I'm not crazy about the terms "target audience" or "best practices" either. But don't get hung up on the vocabulary. Focus instead on the meaning, which I'll try to illuminate as we go along.

REALITY 2: THERE IS NO SUCH THING AS THE GENERAL PUBLIC

When I teach nonprofit marketing workshops in person, I often make participants chant this with me in unison so they remember it: "There is no such thing as the general public! There is no such thing as the general public!"

The general public includes *everyone*, from newborns to elders, rich and poor, incarcerated and homeless. No matter how much you try, you will not reach everyone. In fact, if that's what you try to do, odds are good that you will reach no one. Instead, you need to focus on specific groups of people and work toward communicating with them in ways that connect with their particular needs and values.

When nonprofit marketing programs fail, organizations too frequently blame the tactics. "We tried an email newsletter, but no one read it." "We sent out a direct mail fundraising letter, but it didn't raise much money." Closer examination of those tactics often reveals that the audience was poorly defined and the message was too generic. If the hammer doesn't hit the nail on the head, take a look at the skills of the carpenter, not the hammer.

REALITY 3: YOU NEED TO BUILD YOUR OWN MEDIA EMPIRE

Don't depend on the mainstream media to get your message out. That sector of our society has its own set of survival problems. Instead, consider media relations as just one of your tactics and build your own media empire using affordable online tools.

I'd much rather see a nonprofit spend a day writing blog posts and uploading photos or videos than writing a press release and blasting it out to a hundred reporters. When you publish your own content, you have it forever and can reuse it however you like. You can send it directly to your supporters—and to reporters too. When you write a press release, it may go nowhere. If the media do cover the story, they may pick an entirely different angle or shortchange what you thought was essential. With the larger outlets, the story may be archived behind a paid subscription wall, severely limiting its long-term usefulness to you.

Media coverage can still be incredibly helpful. I'm not suggesting that you forgo media relations entirely. A well-crafted press release sent to a handful of reporters who you know cover your issues can produce great results. If you have good relationships with reporters or work on a subject that's likely to get coverage, by all means take advantage of that. But in today's media environment, with limited time for creating content, I believe you are better off spending more time publishing your own content and, when seeking media coverage, focusing on a highly targeted list of mainstream media outlets.

REALITY 4: ALL GENERATIONS—INCLUDING SENIORS—ARE ONLINE

Great-grandma has email, and she's thinking about getting on Facebook too. After all, her children are telling her it's the best way to keep up with what her younger family members are doing, especially those who live out of town. Too many nonprofits falsely assume that people over sixty-five—who may be their biggest financial supporters—are not online. Although it's true that older generations are not online in the same proportions as younger generations, the gap is closing quickly.

The Pew Internet & American Life Project's "Generations Online in 2009" report found that although eighteen- to forty-four-year-olds account for 53 percent of the total number of Internet users, the biggest increase in Internet use between 2005 and 2008 was within the seventy- to seventy-five-year-old age group. In 2008, more than half of those age sixty-four to sixty-nine—those considered to be in their prime giving years—were online. Three-quarters of Internet users age sixty-four and older send and receive email, making it that age group's most popular online activity. Older users are also more inclined to use the Internet for research (perhaps checking out your website before writing that check), rather than for entertainment, like their grandchildren.

Although social networking is clearly more popular with younger generations, still, one-quarter of Americans fifty-five and older have a Facebook account, according to an April 2009 Harris Interactive poll. In February 2009, Facebook itself reported that its fastest growing demographic was women fifty-five and older.

What's important to remember is that the gaps in Internet use between younger and older generations will continue to close, until they are essentially level. Some of you reading this book (or perhaps some people you work with) might suppose that your particular supporters are in the other half of older Americans who aren't online, and therefore you don't need an online marketing strategy. It's a thin argument, and the holes in it are spreading fast.

Older people will continue to get online; even more significantly, the younger generations—particularly those in their thirties and forties now who came of age with personal computing—will remain online as they age. Their expectations for communicating online with their favorite charities will likely be extremely high. Prepare to meet those demands by getting through the steepest parts of your learning curve now.

REALITY 5: NONPROFIT COMMUNICATORS ARE TRANSFORMING INTO COMMUNITY ORGANIZERS

Although you'll be encouraged in this book to remember that your supporters are real, individual people and to speak to them personally, it's also important to remember the power of your network as a whole and the connections that your supporters have with each other.

Think about when you host events. Isn't it wonderful to see all of those people who care about your work in one place, talking to each other about the good work you are doing, and feeling good about their contributions to something much bigger than themselves?

Smart nonprofit marketers find those people who are enthusiastic about the cause and who also have large networks of their own. You then feed those big fans and help them spread the message to others. They may fundraise for you, but just as important, they also "friendraise" for you.

I believe that the organizations that merge the now separate functions of fundraising, marketing, communications, and information technology into community building or community engagement teams and then incorporate all that is learned through their community of supporters into program design and implementation will ultimately be more successful in the coming years than those who maintain these professional silos.

REALITY 6: PERSONAL AND ORGANIZATIONAL PERSONALITIES, OR BRANDS, ARE BLENDING

What emotions does your nonprofit evoke in people? What is your group known for? This is your organization's brand, image, or personality—and many nonprofits are finding that their organizational brand is closely related to the personalities of their most public staff members. This has always been true for smaller organizations, groups led by a founding or long-time executive director, and nonprofits created in someone else's memory or honor.

But now larger nonprofits must contend with this reality too. Good online marketing, especially in social media, is personal, which means that your staff should present themselves as real human beings in your communications. This mixing of personal and professional can be quite uncomfortable for older generations, but it's a way of life for younger staff members. The personality of the messenger—you—can affect the message. Think about your own personality and voice—your personal brand—and how it impacts the organization's brand.

REALITY 7: GOOD NONPROFIT MARKETING TAKES MORE TIME THAN MONEY

Because the Internet has revolutionized communications between organizations and individuals, effective nonprofit marketing programs can be implemented for online pennies on the print dollar. Although you still need a budget to pay for good web hosting; email service providers; some upgraded, professional-level services; and, of course, staff, lack of money is no longer the biggest stumbling block to good nonprofit marketing. Now the sticking point is lack of time.

Engaging supporters in conversations is more time-consuming than blasting messages out to them. Managing profiles on multiple social media sites is more time-consuming than updating your website once a month. Writing a blog with several posts per week is more time-consuming than sending out a print newsletter twice a year. Although all of these tasks do take more time, they are also more effective at building a community of supporters and encouraging them to act on your behalf.

REALITY 8: YOU'VE ALREADY LOST CONTROL OF YOUR MESSAGE—STOP PRETENDING OTHERWISE

Control over the message about your organization or issue is not yours to give up. It's already gone. What you can control is your response to how others are communicating about your issues and your organization.

One of the most frequent concerns I hear from nonprofits about using social media and participating in conversations with people online is that they fear they will lose control of their messages. They fear people will say bad things or manipulate their image in some way.

It's questionable whether that kind of control ever existed, and when it comes to the Internet, the reality is that it's long gone. If someone wants to bad-mouth you online, they can do it right now whether you are there to see it and respond or not. Turning off your modem (or burying your head in the sand) won't prevent those conversations from happening. They'll just happen without you there to correct any misconceptions.

The truth is that the overwhelming majority of comments that people make about charities online are positive or neutral. For those that are negative, isn't it better to see them and consciously decide whether or not to respond than to be oblivious to them entirely?

Know your controversial or hot-button issues. Anticipate how foes might manipulate your positions, then prepare your response, so you'll be ready should you need to use it. The sheer volume of pro and con voices online does matter. If you are both responding to and initiating positive conversations about your work online, that will balance out, and perhaps even drown out, any negative conversations. But you can't build that fortress of goodwill around you if you aren't participating in the conversation.

A more reasonable goal is consistency in, rather than control of, your messaging. It's much easier to steer a conversation and to suggest topics for additional discussion than it is to control what people say.

REALITY 9: MARKETING IS NOT FUNDRAISING, BUT IT IS ESSENTIAL TO IT

Good nonprofit marketing has many possible outcomes, and raising dollars is one of them. But nonprofits also use marketing to find and galvanize volunteers; to persuade decision makers; to change public policy; to raise awareness; to encourage behavior changes; to converse with clients, supporters, and partners; to foment social change—and more.

Although you can have successful long-term marketing campaigns that don't involve fundraising, you cannot have successful long-term fundraising campaigns without marketing. Marketing and communications are how you talk to your donors in between those times when you ask for money. They're what pull new people into your pool of potential new donors and what keep current donors happy with your organization so they will give again.

This is not a fundraising guide, but you'll find fundraising-related tips and examples throughout the book, because it is one result of successful nonprofit marketing.

REALITY 10: OLD-FASHIONED BASICS STILL WORK BEST, EVEN ONLINE

"The basics are what most organizations are missing. Obsessing about this is far more effective than managing the latest fad." I didn't say that, but I agree with it

100 percent. Marketing guru Seth Godin said it during a May 2008 online chat about nonprofit marketing hosted by the *Chronicle of Philanthropy*.

With online marketing in particular, don't fret about Facebook until your website is in good shape. Don't get all twisted up about Twitter and how many followers you have until your email marketing program is effective and your email list is growing steadily. Focus on the basics first, and do them well.

CONCLUSION: TRY BOLDLY, AND TRY AGAIN

There is no one best way to market your nonprofit or your good cause, although some approaches have better odds of working than others, especially given these ten realities. I've tried to include in this book both the strategies and tactics that I believe will have the greatest likelihood of success for smaller organizations, but you won't know what works best for your group and your supporters until you try, gauge the results, and try again.

Don't fear failure in your nonprofit marketing. Fear will make your approaches too conservative, and you'll become just another one of the thousands of really good causes out there that struggle day to day because they don't get the support they deserve.

Instead, be bold. You won't get it right the first time, and maybe not the second either. What's important is that you try new ways to reach out and grab hold of your supporters' hearts and minds. When you do, they will come to your aid.

chapter
TWO

Nonprofit Marketing Plans in Theory—and in the Real World

It is better to know some of the questions than all of the answers.

—James Thurber

This chapter is about . . .

- The definition of marketing
- A subset of nonprofit marketing called social marketing
- The sections of a comprehensive nonprofit marketing plan
- Three essential questions that make up a quick-and-dirty marketing plan

Many nonprofit leaders, especially those who come to their organizations because of a passionate commitment to a specific cause, mistakenly believe that nonprofit marketing is about nothing more than getting a newsletter out the door a few times a year, updating the website, or selling tickets to a fundraiser. Others, often with more of a nonprofit management or fundraising background, sometimes confuse nonprofit marketing with brand advertising and believe it's all about maintaining the nonprofit's public image. In fact, marketing is much, much more than either of these assumptions.

In this chapter, we'll review a more complete definition of marketing and how it applies to the nonprofit world. We'll examine an important subset of nonprofit marketing called "social marketing," as well as the sections of a comprehensive nonprofit marketing plan. Then we'll compare that comprehensive model to a simplified quick-and-dirty approach that works better for smaller organizations or anyone in a hurry.

THE REAL DEFINITION OF MARKETING

Consider this official definition of marketing from the American Marketing Association: "Marketing is the activity, set of institutions, and processes for creating, communicating, delivering, and exchanging offerings that have value for customers, clients, partners, and society at large." It's much more than just *communicating* about the programs or services that your nonprofit provides. Marketing is also about *creating* those programs or services, from the outset, and *delivering* them to your participants and supporters. Thus marketing is not just something you do when you have the time or money; it's an essential component of a well-run organization, right alongside strategic planning, financial management, and evaluation of your effectiveness in implementing your mission.

Also included in the formal definition of marketing is *exchanging offerings that have value*—in simpler terms, you give a valuable to someone and you get one from them in return. In the business world, a person gives money to a business and the business gives them a service or product, like a box of cereal. But long before you walk out of the grocery store with a box of Crunchy Cocoa Flakes, the business's marketing department has helped determine how that cereal tastes and what it looks like in the bowl, because they have learned all about the cereal preferences of people that make up families like yours. They've figured out how much to charge you for it, based not on production costs alone but also on what they think you'd be willing to pay. They've also decided which stores will carry the cereal on their shelves. They've figured out what the box should look like and what they need to put in the TV commercials so your kids will drive you crazy until you add Crunchy Cocoa Flakes to the shopping list.

Of course, it's not quite that simple in the nonprofit world.

Instead of boxes of cereal, nonprofits are often "selling" products and services that are much more abstract, such as education, advocacy, facilitation, technical assistance, and networking. Many times the characteristics and descriptions of those products and services are not solely for the nonprofit to decide; they are defined instead by government agencies, foundations, and other institutions that fund or regulate the nonprofit's programs.

The exchange is also not as simple as swiping a debit card and walking out of a store with a bag full of groceries. In the nonprofit world, programs are often offered to individuals for free, because their creation is paid for by contracts, grants, or other charitable donations. The individual participants pay for what's offered with something other than money, such as their time, by performing a desired action, or simply by demonstrating a willingness to consider a different point of view.

In addition to these costs to both the nonprofit and the participants, we must also consider what's called the "benefit exchange." What does the nonprofit get out of it, and what does the participant get out of it? Where is the real value to both parties? Nonprofits often get one step closer to achieving their mission, whether it's reducing domestic violence or beautifying a neighborhood. Participants, on the other hand, often get some kind of emotional payback, such as feeling physically safer or knowing they've made their community a better place for their children.

THE FIVE PS OF SOCIAL MARKETING

Often nonprofits are trying to get people to change their behavior in some way to bring about some greater social good. To translate the concepts of for-profit marketing for financial rewards to nonprofit marketing for social good, the concept of "social marketing" was born.

Social marketing is defined as using marketing concepts and techniques to achieve specific behavioral goals for a social good. Don't confuse it with "social networking," which typically refers to online communities like Facebook, or with "social media marketing," which refers to using Web 2.0 tools like blogs, online video, and other social media (including social networking sites) to market a product or service.

The majority of social marketers work in public health and safety and use social marketing to get people to stop smoking, eat a healthier diet, wear seatbelts, and the like. Professionals in other fields who seek widespread behavior changes, such as environmentalists who want people to carpool and recycle more, are also adopting this methodology. Social marketing is not for every nonprofit; it makes sense to use this particular approach only when you are trying to convince individuals within your target audience to change their behaviors for some greater social good. If you are trying to market more traditional products or services—such as convincing state lawmakers to embrace your suggested policy reforms (a product) or getting seniors to sign up for Meals on Wheels (a service)—you can still learn from this approach, but you will not use it explicitly to outline your marketing plan.

Social marketing practitioners use the "five Ps of social marketing" to structure their marketing plans, the first four of which originate directly from what's often called "the marketing mix" or the "four Ps of marketing" in the for-profit world.

Product. The behavior you want to bring about and any items needed to support that behavior. In other words, what do you want people to do and what items do they need in order to do it?

Price. What is the cost to make this behavior change, including money, time, status, inconvenience, social stigma, and so on? Price is very closely related to the values of your specific target audience. Is it worth it?

Place. Where does this behavior change need to take place? When are people thinking about it? How do the surroundings help or hurt?

Promotion. What messages will make sense to your target audience and how should they be delivered?

Policy. What policies, rules, or requirements help or hurt when trying to change behaviors?

To help you see how the five Ps of social marketing fit into a more traditional nonprofit marketing plan structure for a product or service, you'll see references to each P in the various sections of the plan.

ELEMENTS OF A COMPREHENSIVE NONPROFIT MARKETING PLAN

You now understand that marketing is much more than your image or a set of communications tactics. If you are interested in convincing individuals to change their behaviors in some way, you've seen how social marketers use the five Ps to outline a strategy. Now let's take a look at the elements of a comprehensive marketing strategy that you could use to market a campaign, a program, a product, an event, or a service of your organization to clients, participants, or attendees (see Table 2.1). You could also use this type of plan to market your organization as a whole to supporters like volunteers and donors.

Marketing Goals

In this section, you define what you need to do or to accomplish.

What are your short-term and long-term goals? What do you want to achieve through marketing? What is your *product*—what are you "selling" to participants, clients, or supporters? What are you trying to get people to do? What kind of installment plan or baby steps can people take toward full acceptance of your product? What are the advantages of the product? Is it compatible with social norms? Is it simple to understand? Can you see someone doing it?

Environmental Analysis

Here you describe the conditions under which you must operate. This is also called an environmental scan or situational analysis. You'll also sometimes see

Table 2.1.
Elements of a Comprehensive Marketing Plan

Plan Section	What Goes in It
Marketing Goals	What you need to do or accomplish; what actions you need others to take
Environmental Analysis	The conditions under which you must operate
Audience and Segmentation	Who you must reach and convince, their interests and values
Messaging	The specific messages that will move your audience to action
Marketing Tactics	How you will deliver your messages
Short-Term Steps	Actions you should take in the first few months
Long-Term Steps	Actions you will take later
Budget and Staffing	Resources required to implement the plan
Strategy Metrics	How you will measure progress against your goals

a SWOT analysis—a review of the strengths, weaknesses, opportunities, and threats associated with the product—here too.

What are the internal conditions under which your marketing program must operate? What are the external conditions under which you must operate? What resources are available within your organization? What partnerships can you rely on? What skills do you need and which do you have on staff now? What systems need to be in place in order for your plan to succeed? What barriers must be overcome for your plan to be successful?

Who is the competition—who else is providing similar resources and information? Who is providing information or urging actions that are in conflict with your approach? Are there any myths that must be overcome? Are there any *policies* that will positively affect the outcome of your marketing plan? Are there any policies that could negatively affect the success of the marketing strategy?

Audience and Segmentation

In this section, you describe in great detail who you are communicating with and what their interests and needs are.

What groups of people are you trying to reach? Within those groups, what are the specific subgroups of people who are most important to you? Who are some personas within the groups? What do these people care about? What's important to them? What's not important to them? What is their current level of interest in you and your issues? How much knowledge do they already have? What else do you believe they need to know?

What are the *prices* your target audience must pay for accepting your product? What barriers are in their way? What is the benefit exchange—what do they get in return for paying the price for your product?

Where are the *places* that your target audiences go, offline and online? Are there gatekeepers at these places whom you must reach out to first?

Messaging

In this section you lay out the specific messages that are most likely to work with your target audiences.

Given your target audiences' interests, needs, and values, what specific messages about you and your work are most likely to resonate with them? What messages or approaches would they be most likely to ignore? What kind of information do the specific audiences want to receive from you? What messages make the benefit exchange clear? Should you use humor? What metaphors will make sense to your audience? What stories can you tell to provide inspiration or instruction?

Marketing Tactics

Here you describe the tactics you will use to deliver your messages to your audiences.

What communications tools should you use to deliver messages to the target audiences? How specific and personalized should communications be? Who should deliver the message? Can partners help? Will you use offline tactics, online tactics, or a combination? What role will various tactics like word-of-mouth, advertising, and media coverage play? How often should your audiences receive the messages via any given communications channel? Where should these messages appear? Where will your audiences be when they hear or see them? When will your audience be most receptive to hearing the messages? In other words, how will you promote your product?

Short-Term Steps

This is your specific, short-term action plan. What specific steps should you take quickly (say, within the next six months) to implement the strategy?

Long-Term Steps

This is your specific, long-term action plan. What specific steps should you take beyond the next six months to implement the strategy?

Budget and Staffing

In this section, you outline the financial and staffing resources required to implement the plan.

What financial resources are required? Where will these resources come from? Do they exist today or do they need to be developed? What staffing resources are required? Do you have the skills and time needed on staff? Or do you need to hire new staff and consultants/freelancers? Do you need to recruit volunteers to perform certain tasks? Do you need to enlist the support of various partners to implement parts of the action plan?

What elements of the plan will be scaled back first if adequate resources are not available? What elements of the plan should be expanded or accelerated first should additional resources become available?

Strategy Metrics

Here you describe how you will measure the impact of your communications tactics to see how well you are achieving your goals.

What specific measures are available to track the effectiveness of the marketing campaign? Which measures are of primary importance and which are secondary? How often will you review and report on the metrics? How will the metrics influence adjustments to the plan? What's impossible to measure, but still important to consider, perhaps through anecdotal information? Are there any unstated or hidden expectations that need to be addressed?

NONPROFIT MARKETING THE QUICK-AND-DIRTY WAY

Although drafting a comprehensive marketing plan that answers the scores of questions posed here is ideal, the reality is that this kind of thoughtful, well-researched, and well-considered plan is out of the reach of many organizations, perhaps including yours, because you simply don't have the money, time, or staff to pull it off. If so, you'll turn instead to the quick-and-dirty approach that focuses on the three most important questions in nonprofit marketing:

Who are we trying to reach? Define your target audience.

What's our message to them? Explain what you want them to do and why they should do it, or why they should care.

What's the best way to deliver that message? Pick the right channels to deliver your message to your target audience.

Part Two is devoted to creating a quick-and-dirty marketing plan, with Chapters Four, Five, and Six covering each of these three questions respectively.

EXAMPLE: THE AMERICAN RED CROSS'S "DO MORE THAN CROSS YOUR FINGERS" CAMPAIGN

The American Red Cross wants every household to do three things: to get an emergency kit, to make a communication and evacuation plan, and to be informed about the disasters that are common in their communities. That's their product. Fair enough, but how are they going to make it happen?

Although the American Red Cross has the resources to develop comprehensive marketing strategies complete with healthy amounts of audience research and environmental analyses, I asked Mark Ferguson, who manages the "Do More Than Cross Your Fingers" campaign and other corporate partnerships for the American Red Cross, to share the marketing strategy for the campaign in the quick-and-dirty format.[1]

Defining the Audience: Moms with Kids at Home

The Red Cross's historical research and experience shows that moms with kids under eighteen living at home are especially receptive to messages about disaster preparedness. No surprise there—if anyone is going to care about the nest and the babies in it, it's Mom. But some recent research also shows that 82 percent of moms say they drive household purchases. So if you are trying to get a family to organize a disaster preparedness kit that will most likely require some purchases, reaching out to the people who decide what to buy makes sense.

Creating the Message: Testing the Campaign Slogan

But what do you say to a busy mom to get her to make this a priority? It was important for the Red Cross to come up with a message that spoke to moms but that also had broader appeal to the American public at large. Even if moms were the target, the message needed to be appropriate for a much wider audience as well. It was also important, says Mark, for the message to start from where people are now and to help them move forward with their family disaster planning, regardless of how much they may have already done. Through their research, they knew that about 80 percent of families had taken one of the three key steps (getting a kit, making a plan, or staying informed), and this campaign was about moving them to take another.

To come up with the right message, the Red Cross hired the firm Catchword Branding, which specializes in naming. They provided a thousand possible slogans to the Red Cross, many of which were simple variations on one idea. Using a cross-functional team (marketing, development, disaster preparedness, field staff, and so on), the Red Cross whittled the list down to the best five. Those five were then tested through an online survey with Harris Interactive to find which one resonated best both with moms and with the public at large.

Of the five options, says Mark, one was in the form of a question and one played on the "heroes" theme that the Red Cross has used successfully before. Another one was deemed too snarky or too clever (survey respondents said it just didn't sound like the Red Cross). The chosen theme, Do More Than Cross

Your Fingers, stood out among the five with both moms and the public at large. "It was fresh," says Mark, "but not in any way offensive."

Delivering the Message: Going Where Moms Are and Using Voices They Trust

With a message in hand, the next decision was how to get it out to moms. "We know that moms are really active online," says Mark, quoting a 2009 Nielsen survey that said 20 percent of the active online population are moms aged twenty-five to fifty-four with at least one child living at home. Thus the campaign centers on www.redcross.org/domore, and all of the other online and offline tactics will point back to that page.

The Red Cross also wanted to emphasize that each family is different, so what's in their emergency kits should be different too. Thus one of the key components of the website is a game called Prepare 4 that helps you build your own personalized kit.

"One of the goals is to make disaster preparedness simple and interesting," says Mark, "Not just a brochure or a ho-hum shopping list. We wanted something interactive and friendly." During the game, you answer questions that help you build a kit that's customized for your family, right down to including something fun for the kids to do while the power is out. At the end of the game, your list of items is emailed to you so that you can go gather up the items from around your house and go shopping for what's missing.

You can also share what you are including in your personal kit with others in the My Kit section, as spokesperson Jamie Lee Curtis has done on the site via video. The selection of Curtis as the spokesperson is another move that connects well with moms.

The Red Cross also reached out to "mommy bloggers" (one of the biggest forces in the blogosphere) who have blogged about disaster preparedness before. They pursued coverage in traditional print magazines focused on women and parenting. Marketing partnerships with Clorox (a brand many moms use daily) and FedEx (many moms also run small businesses, and FedEx is already reaching out to NASCAR-watching moms with the preparedness message) round out the campaign channels.

The Red Cross will evaluate the effectiveness of the campaign through annual surveys on how well prepared American households are for a disaster.

CONCLUSION: ALWAYS THINK BEFORE YOU SPEAK

No matter how big or how small your nonprofit may be, asking yourself the three basic questions behind a quick-and-dirty marketing plan will help ensure that you are headed in the right direction:

- Who are we trying to reach?
- What's our message to them?
- What's the best way to deliver that message?

Creating a marketing plan *before* launching into tactics, however simple the plan (even if it's nothing more than answers to these questions on the back of a napkin), is always a smart approach. It's as true for nonprofit marketing as it is for disaster preparedness—you have to do more than cross your fingers!

chapter THREE

Listen to the World Around You

Wisdom is the reward for a lifetime of listening . . . when you'd have preferred to talk.

—D. J. Kaufman

This chapter is about . . .

- The importance of listening in marketing
- Offline and online strategies and tools for listening
- How to use what you learn by listening to improve your marketing

Whether you call it listening, intelligence gathering, or market research, you need to pay attention to what's happening in the world around you. Your nonprofit doesn't operate in a bubble, so pretending that it does will only hurt your organization and make it impossible to successfully market your cause.

This advice—to listen before you speak—may sound like simple etiquette, but it's really about much more than that. A good listening network should serve as a cornerstone of not just your marketing program, but also how you manage your entire nonprofit organization. What you learn through listening should shape the way you approach your mission and how you design and implement all of your various programs—not just your marketing or fundraising. Listening helps at every level: it can help your professional community thrive, your organization prosper, your individual programs grow, and your own personal career soar.

Every day presents an opportunity to learn more about the people you are trying to help and the people who are trying to help you. If you listen closely, you will learn a great deal from the simple personal interactions that take place in and around the office every day. But in addition to this ambient listening, you should also put in place a more formal listening structure or network that allows you to keep the two-way flow of information between you and others open and moving.

Your listening network should include both in-person and online tools. It should include data generated by others (such as national polling data) and data you create specifically for your organization (such as evaluation forms that participants complete after an event). Web 2.0, or social media, allows people to connect, converse, and collaborate with others more easily, regardless of time zones or geographic boundaries. Several online tools allow you to tap into these online conversations to learn even more about how people feel about your cause and your organization.

WATCH AND LISTEN

When getting to know a group of people, whether they are program participants or major donors to your cause, nothing works better than talking directly to members of that group. Although formal focus groups with two-way mirrors and trained facilitators or national telephone surveys may be some of the most effective ways to learn about your target audience, they are also very expensive. Don't consider formal research unless you have a minimum of $10,000 to spend. The good news is that informal research, which is either free or affordable, works just as well for most organizations.

To learn more about a particular group of people, simply go talk to some people who fit the description of that group. Hang out where they are. In every conversation that you strike up, ask a few questions that help you learn more about what's important to them, what their days are like, what infuriates them, and what makes them laugh. Get to know them as people, before you start to think of them as potential clients or supporters.

Do the same kind of watching and listening with your current clients and supporters. Take them out to lunch and learn everything you can about these people.

Ask them directly: What is it about your nonprofit or your cause that motivates them to be involved? What is it about your nonprofit that your donors, volunteers, and other supporters find so compelling? The answers may surprise you.

For example, I'm on the board of a local HIV/AIDS support organization. At a meeting shortly after I joined the board, each of us explained why he or she wanted to serve on this board. Being new and knowing only a few other board members before this meeting, I suspected that the majority would give reasons related to disease prevention or to a personal experience with HIV or AIDS.

Although that was certainly a motivation for several people in the room, most of us (including me) focused instead on wanting to fight for the underdog, the people society would rather turn away from. It wasn't HIV, per se, that motivated us as much as the impact of the stigma of HIV on people in the Southern rural counties where the nonprofit operates, and our desire to fight that discrimination. If we polled our donors and other supporters, I suspect we'd hear similar comments.

Hearing perspectives like these from your target audience can be incredibly helpful when it comes time to sit down and write a newsletter or a fundraising appeal letter, or to recruit new members to the board. It gives you a big head start in creating messages that will appeal directly to their values.

CONVENE INFORMAL FOCUS GROUPS

You don't need a two-way mirrored conference room to hold a focus group. Instead, invite six to twelve people to come by your office. Better yet, find a location closer to where they are. Offer them a meal during the day or dessert and coffee at night. It's easier to draw conclusions from informal focus groups if everyone in the room is a member of a particular target audience group that you have previously defined (for example, limited to parents of high school students you hope will enroll in your after-school driver safety program, rather than including people without children or with only very young children).

Develop a discussion guide of four to six questions per hour, up to two hours per session. Broad questions about experiences, like "Tell me what happens when . . ." and "What would you do if . . ." can get the conversation going, without pointing it in too specific a direction. Make sure your focus group facilitator understands the issues and questions but can remain completely neutral during the discussions. It's important that the participants don't think you are looking for particular answers. They may want to please you and tell you what you want to hear.

In most cases you'll want to record the session so you can review it again later. It's also helpful to ask participants to make their own notes about the questions you are asking before the conversation really begins, so you have a record of those first impressions as well.

Sarah Durham, founder of Big Duck, a nonprofit communications consulting firm in New York City, often works with clients to conduct informal focus groups. One client, a community development organization that served the residents of several public housing developments and ran numerous social service programs, had a problem: the people who were using their services the most didn't live in the particular public housing developments they were targeting. Although people were using their employment assistance programs, they weren't the people they were trying to reach.

To find out why the right people—the public housing residents—weren't using the programs, Big Duck helped the organization conduct five informal focus groups. The focus groups were to be held in the on-site community centers in each development, and a few days before the focus groups, program staff actively recruited residents to attend. Participants received a free dinner and discussed the kind of services they needed and what they knew about the nonprofit organization.

As they talked with the residents, the organizers had what Sarah calls a big "Aha!" moment. The nonprofit had been using traditional advertising methods to spread the word about their free programs, including advertising on garbage cans, posting flyers, and hiring people to hand out postcards describing the services they offer. What they heard in the informal focus groups was that the residents were suspicious of anything marketed as "free" by people who appeared to be strangers. They figured there had to be a catch, so they ignored the advertising.

In response to what they learned through these focus groups, the nonprofit completely shifted its marketing away from the blitz of generic outreach and toward more personal one-on-one testimonials from current program participants. They found that the most effective way to bring a new participant into the program was to have a current participant share her or his success story with that person and to accompany them to the program office.

The nonprofit now also holds block parties where people who have graduated from the program speak about their experiences and bring their friends. Not only is the new approach more effective in recruiting the right people, but it also costs less than the old way of hiring people to stand around thrusting postcards toward passersby.

CONDUCT ONLINE SURVEYS

If you have a good email list or a large enough web or social media presence, you can use free or affordable online survey tools to collect data. Online surveys allow you to easily calculate quantitative (numerical) data by seeing how many people answer multiple choice questions in a particular way or rank various choices. You can also collect qualitative data (anecdotes) through open-ended text boxes. Although these are harder to compile, it allows your survey respondents to answer in their own words, which gives you valuable insight into the vocabulary they use and the way they describe certain situations.

Perhaps the biggest challenge with online surveys is ensuring that your questions are not leading or loaded. In other words, you don't want the way your question is worded to push respondents toward one answer over another. Online survey providers often supply tips to their customers on how to write good questions and how to use their tools most effectively.

Be sure to collect demographic data as well, such as gender, age, or location. This allows you to analyze your data in different ways so you can compare how different subsets of your target audience responded to your questions.

ANALYZE YOUR WEB AND EMAIL STATISTICS

You can also learn a great deal about your website visitors and email newsletter subscribers by studying your website and email analytics—an analysis of the statistics associated with your website and email programs. In particular, look at the search terms people are using to get to your site from places like Google. A basic website statistics program, which is typically included in your website hosting package, will show you which pages they are staying on the longest and the pages through which they entered and exited your site. Your email newsletter service provider can tell you how many people are clicking on various links in your newsletter, signaling which topics people are most interested in.

REVIEW MEDIA KITS AND ADVERTISING

Media kits can also be very helpful. If you know that your target audience reads a particular publication or uses a certain website, obtain the media kit for that publication or site, which you can often find online in the "About," "Advertising," or "Partners" section of a media outlet's website. Media kits show potential advertisers the demographic information about the readers of that publication or users of the website. They are trying to convince advertisers to pay them money in return for reaching a certain demographic. You can use this same data to better understand those people in your target audience who read that publication. Media kits are often available online, although you sometimes need to request one directly from the advertising sales department.

WATCH FOR RELEVANT POLLING AND SURVEY DATA

Many national polling and survey companies now share data online. Excellent sources for the nonprofit sector include the Pew Internet and American Life Project and Harris Interactive. For more suggestions on where to obtain free or affordable polling and survey data related to your target audience, visit the companion website.

UNFAMILIAR WITH SOME OF THE TERMS IN THIS CHAPTER?

If you find some of the terminology in this section foreign or confusing, refer to the Glossary of Online Marketing Terms at the back of the book.

MONITOR ONLINE MENTIONS AND SOCIAL MEDIA CONVERSATIONS

By performing keyword searches with online search and monitoring tools, you can find and keep track of what's being said on websites (including news sites), blogs, social networking sites like Facebook and Twitter, online bulletin boards, and more.

Develop Your Keyword List

The first step in creating your online listening network is to develop a list of keywords that you can feed into various search engines, which will then return content to you that contains those words.

Some keyword choices will be obvious:

- Your organization's name and any common shortened versions or acronyms
- Names of your flagship programs, services, and events
- Names of your executive director and other leaders and "public faces" of the organization
- URL for your website(s)
- Your tagline or program slogans

Next, consider the competition. Which organizations in your community (geographic, professional, or topical) are reaching out to the same neighbors, media contacts, business leaders and other potential supporters for assistance? Who is also communicating about the same issues that your organization does, with either similar or opposing points of view, regardless of whether they are local, regional, or national organizations? Consider adding the names of these "friend" and "enemy" organizations (and the "frenemies" in between), perhaps paired with some specific topical keywords, to your list.

You should also track keywords related to the kind of work you do. Add the terms that describe your mission area and programmatic focus to your list, putting exact phrases, like names, in quotations marks. This is the area that will require the most refinement so that you end up seeing results you really care most about. You might pick a handful of keywords to get started and adjust from there. A humane society might track keywords like "humane society," "animal shelter," "lost dog," and "adopt a pet."

To go one step further, think about what are called "long-tail keywords." These are actually phrases of multiple words, often repeating in different orders. Although fewer people may be using these more specific terms, they are likely to be more closely related to the work you do. For example, long-tail versions of a humane society's keywords could include geographic descriptions like "Chicago humane society," "humane society Chicago," and "Illinois humane society," as well as more complete descriptions of what a person might be talking about online, such as "how to find a dog that ran away," or "create a flyer for a lost dog."

Google's External Keyword Tool (search for Google External Keyword Tool to find it) will help you identify alternate phrases that searchers are using related to your original keywords. For example, when you enter "lost pet" into the Keyword Tool, you'll see that "find lost pet" and "found lost pet" are common search phrases, representing people who have both lost *and* found pets.

You can also use Google's Keyword Tool to find out the keywords used by other organizations. If you find a website within your professional community that is highly ranked in the Google search results, go back to the Keyword Tool and run the site's URL through the tool. Google will return the keywords it associates with that site. Also take some time to explore Google Trends and Google Insights, which will let you compare search terms against each other and compare search volume patterns across regions, categories, and time frames. You can also use the www.Delicious.com "Look Up a URL" search to learn about the words other people are using to tag your content. By entering the URL of a web page, you can see what words people who saved the page to Delicious used to tag it.

Set Up Your Searches

With your keyword list in hand, you are ready to enter them into several different search engines so you can see who is talking about your keywords, what they are saying, and where they are saying it. Although setting up your online listening network is easy, it does take some time to get the network humming in a tune you can understand. Don't be discouraged by the amount of information or noise that you get back from these searches, whether it seems like too much or too little. Expect to tinker with your keywords, the way you collect and review what those searches return, and how you analyze it, until you find the right frequency.

Many free and affordable tools are available to help you find and manage all of this information. Professional tools go a few steps further by sifting and organizing the information for you and making some judgments about whether the sentiment about your organization is positive, neutral, or negative, for example.

Start by setting up an RSS reader, such as Google Reader. This allows you to subscribe not only to blogs and other RSS feeds, but to searches as well. Any page that displays the RSS icon—a white "radio waves" image on an orange square—offers a feed that you can subscribe to in your reader. Next, set up Google Alerts and set an alert for each of your keywords. You can choose to receive the alert via email or feed (I highly recommend the feed, which you'll subscribe to in Google Reader). Do the same thing at other sites that you want to search regularly:

- Twitter.com (run the search for your keyword, then click "RSS feed for this query")
- BoardReader.com (run the search, then click "Tools" and "Subscribe")
- LinkedIn.com (you can subscribe to broad categories in the "Answers" section and via email to discussions within groups you have joined)

You can also experiment with SocialMention.com. You can select different types of social media channels or "All," which will produce some overlap with what you find through Google Alerts and Twitter searches. Again, subscribe to the RSS feed for this search. Try to check your reader a couple of times per week, if not daily.

Until you have a better sense for the volume of information you'll be receiving, I recommend starting with these free tools. Once you are comfortable with the process of reviewing the data that comes in, sign up for free trials of some of the paid services and compare what they find to what the free tools produce. Review whether the analysis provided by the paid tools is helpful or insightful enough to warrant the fee. Based on your comparison, decide whether an upgrade makes sense. Visit the companion website for recommendations on specific listening tools.

FOLLOW SPECIFIC PEOPLE AND SOURCES ONLINE

Once you've been listening for a while through your keyword searches, you can develop a list of people who often talk about issues you care about and start following them directly. Subscribe to their blogs in your reader, follow them on Twitter, and become a Facebook friend or fan of their Facebook page. The same goes for specific places on the web, such as news sites or blogs with multiple authors.

To keep track of your top blogs and bloggers, I highly recommend that you create your own page at Alltop.com, which calls itself an online magazine rack. When you create your own page, you select the blogs that you want to follow, and the last five headlines from each of those blogs appears all on one page. When I'm too busy to read my RSS reader, I scan my Alltop page instead: my.alltop.com/kivilm. Alltop also groups blogs into hundreds of categories—for example, animal rescue, hunger, and literacy—some of which may be related to your mission.

WHAT TO DO WITH WHAT YOU LEARN

Here are seventeen concrete actions you can take, using what you learn from listening.

1. *Better understand the people who matter most.* Find, follow, and listen to the people who you think match your target audience, whether they are potential clients, funders, donors, advocates, or volunteers. Learn more about what interests them, what kinds of questions they have, and the language they use, so you can communicate with them in more meaningful ways. It's basic market research, and if you listen for no other reason, you will still find it worthwhile.

2. *Start conversations with potential new supporters.* See who's talking about your issues. Look at what else those people are saying online. If you think these are individuals who would be interested in what your organization does, reach out to them with a personal message. Offer information or resources or invite them to an event. Open the door to a relationship, just as you would to a personal friendship.

3. *Answer questions and provide suggestions.* On social media and networking sites people are constantly posing questions and talking about the challenges they face. Answer questions, offer suggestions, and become known as a good source of information and assistance.

4. *Correct misconceptions.* Is someone confused, misinformed, or worse, spreading rumors? Try to set the record straight by presenting your point of view in a nonconfrontational way.

5. *Find new partners.* Discover who else is interested in and working on the same things you are, especially people and organizations you otherwise might never have known existed (for example, they do what you do, but on the other side of the country). Share your successes, replicate theirs, and create new partnerships to get more done.

6. *Measure the success of your communications.* Are you trying to get the word out? See how well the message is spreading by monitoring who's passing it on to others and how the message is changing as it spreads.

7. *Feed your biggest fans.* Build personal relationships with your biggest fans and give them what they need to spread the word about you (for example, great stories, photos, videos, inside scoops on what's happening in your field). These are the people who will not only introduce you to their friends and expand your circle of supporters but also stand up and defend you and your cause if attacked by others, so keep them on your side.

8. *Increase your own professional knowledge.* Identify the leaders and big thinkers (I call them the "big brains") in your field; keep an eye on the issues they are discussing and the resources they are recommending. It's like attending a professional networking event without leaving your desk.

9. *Keep tabs on your critics.* Even if you choose not to respond directly now, keeping up with what your critics are saying will help you develop better rebuttals and fine-tune your messaging in the future.

10. *Find your niche.* It's a competitive world, even for nonprofits (some might say *especially* for nonprofits when financial times are tough). By listening to what's going on in your professional world, you'll have a much better understanding of where you fit in, where you can fill gaps, and how you can stand out. And you *must* stand out—that's what nonprofit marketing is ultimately all about.

11. *Knock down your writer's block.* Not sure what to write about in your newsletter or blog? Read what others in your community are talking about and then write about the trends you see, draft a response to something you found particularly interesting or offensive, or summarize the best points others are making on a particular topic.

12. *Pick up a reality check.* We all make assumptions every day, but when you assume too much, you know what happens? "You make an *ass* out of *u* and *me*." (I thought that was so profound when I figured it out at age ten!) Road test your assumptions by putting them out there and listening to the responses you get.

13. *Spot programmatic trends earlier.* By consistently listening to the "raw feed," you'll be able to pick up on trends related to your work long before they solidify into conventional wisdom. You can adjust your programs accordingly, and when others finally catch up, you'll be considered on the cutting edge.

14. *Respond rapidly to flare-ups.* Listening puts you higher up in your own personal fire tower, so when a potential firestorm sparks, you can douse the flames much faster than if you were on the ground, miles away.

15. *Learn the lingo.* Learn what words your target audience is using. The language that your clients use, for example, is often very different from the language that professionals in the field use. The reverse is true too: if you are trying to break into a professional community, listening is a good way to pick up on some of their jargon and buzzwords.

16. *Be relevant.* If you want to be considered a player in the space you are working in, you have to be relevant. And to be relevant, you have to understand where people are *right now.* Listening helps you keep up with what's happening to the people who matter to your organization's success.

17. *Give good customer service.* If your nonprofit is in the business of providing direct services, the people you serve are not unlike customers at a commercial establishment. A growing number of commercial brands, like Dell and Comcast, are listening on a near-constant, real-time basis to answer customer questions and address complaints.

HOW TO HANDLE CRANKS, TROLLS, AND FLAMERS

When you start listening to online conversations, you may find that not everything you hear is flattering. Although the majority of what you hear will probably be positive or neutral (unless you work on controversial social issues), you'll also run into the occasional and dreaded trolls, cranks, and flamers.

Although each of these Internet pests has its own definition, their basic motivation is the same: getting attention. The troll will try to encourage chaos among your blog readers by leaving rude comments. The crank may try to discourage others from backing your cause. The flamer will attempt to rile you up with personal attacks. They may go about it in different ways, but it's all with the same end in mind: "Notice me!" Whether you respond to them or ignore them depends on where the comment appears and what you believe the impact of the comment will be.

If you publish your own blog, establish a comment policy. Let readers know exactly what you expect from them when they comment and what you will and will not condone. Keep it simple and stick to it. If your blog has the option, do not allow anonymous posting.

So what to do if these pests invade your blog? Don't feed the troll. Simply put, ignore the person and ask your regular posters to do the same. They are just looking for a response, any response, so don't give it to them. Even deleting their comment satisfies their hunger and should be done only if the comment is truly offensive. If they continue to plague your site, be swift with retribution. Your blog should allow you to ban the IP addresses of trolls. This way your blog will recognize their computer, not a username, which can easily be changed.

Before you start deleting comments, be sure that what you are dealing with is actually a troll. Just because someone disagrees with you doesn't mean what they are saying isn't worthy of discussion. Diverging viewpoints among readers offer a great way to encourage conversation, which should be a primary goal of your blog. Healthy debate is great for fostering community and will make your blog a safe place where ideas can be discussed openly. Proceed with extreme caution when it comes to banning and deleting.

Finally, if you feel that you just can't ignore a comment, be careful in your response. Step away from the computer. Don't respond in anger, no matter how upsetting the comment is. Take some time and formulate a rational response. Disarm the crank by being positive. Find something of merit in what was said and start with that.

What about comments that appear on other people's blogs? Although deleting them will not be an option, you should go through the same kind of decision making. Sometimes ignoring a comment is the best approach, especially if others are ignoring it too. Let it die. You can also ignore it if you feel like others are handling it adequately through their own responses. If you decide to respond, do so thoughtfully and respectfully.

CONCLUSION: NEVER STOP LISTENING

By listening to the world around you, including conversations online, you'll have a much better understanding of what's happening in your field, and you'll know where you should engage in conversations with supporters and other people important to your success. Listen to learn who's talking about your issues and your organization, where the buzz is building, and what your supporters are excited about, whether you ever see these people in person or not. People are talking about the issues you care about and even about your organization and staff. The question is whether you'll listen in and how you'll respond to what you hear.

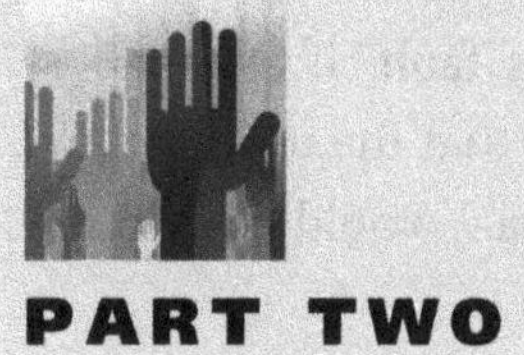

PART TWO

Writing a Quick-and-Dirty Marketing Plan for a Specific Program

Ari Wallach, co-executive director of the Jewish Council for Education and Research (JCER), a political action committee, was surprised to see Barack Obama hovering at only 60 percent of the Jewish vote in summer 2008 polls. In past presidential elections, Jews have overwhelmingly chosen the more progressive candidate. JCER had created JewsVote.org to support its advocacy for Obama, but after seeing these lower-than-expected polling numbers, Wallach knew they needed to do something more.

By using connections and keeping it simple, JCER produced TheGreatSchlep.com, including the now infamous video featuring comedian

Sarah Silverman, for less than $50,000.[1] In the video, Silverman recalls how "Gore got f***** by Florida" and how it would be "the Jews' fault" if Obama lost the election. And those were the tame parts. It's fair to say that the ultimate target audience for this campaign—older Jews living in Florida—would have found the video distasteful, if not completely appalling.

But the video wasn't created for them. It was created for their twenty-something grandchildren—young, progressive, Comedy Central–loving Jews with contacts in Florida—who Wallach saw as the ideal carriers of the pro-Obama message. It worked. The site went viral, was covered by the major networks, and raised more than $250,000 in less than four months. But more important, it mobilized thousands of young Jews to talk to their grandparents about Obama. According to the national exit polls, Jews voted for Obama over McCain 78 percent to 21 percent, and he won Florida convincingly.

This campaign was wildly successful because it targeted a very specific audience important to the cause (older, progressive Jews living in the battleground state of Florida who were hesitant to vote for Obama), with a message that was meaningful to them (Obama is the best chance for a president who supports the same policies that they do), delivered in a package they couldn't resist (a visit, or at least a call, from their grandchildren).

That's what you need to do too, but in your own way, and probably minus the profanity.

Unfortunately, many nonprofits are still pursuing outreach strategies for the general public that are, generally and predictably, a failure. They are so afraid they might offend someone that they end up impressing no one. In Part Two, you'll learn how to create a nonprofit marketing strategy for a particular program, project, campaign, or service of your organization the quick-and-dirty way, by focusing on the three most important questions every marketing plan should answer. You'll learn how to define your audience (Chapter Four), create a powerful message (Chapter Five), and deliver that message to your audience (Chapter Six). You'll also learn about the power of storytelling to spread your message even further (Chapter Seven).

chapter
FOUR

Define Your Audiences: Who Do You Want to Reach?

I don't know the key to success, but the key to failure is trying to please everybody.

—Bill Cosby

This chapter is about . . .

- Recognizing your multiple target audiences
- Segmenting your audiences into groups
- Creating personas to describe your groups
- Focusing on your audience's needs and values

The first step in creating any nonprofit marketing strategy is defining who it is you are trying to reach. The alternative—skipping this step and creating outreach and fundraising campaigns for the general public—is a complete waste of time.

The reality is that most people will never, ever care about your mission enough to help your organization. The general public includes high-school seniors and octogenarians. It includes single moms living on public assistance and business moguls living in high-rise penthouses. It includes liberals, conservatives, and people who have never voted in their lives and probably never will. They should all care, every single one of them, about child abuse, global warming, and your good cause too. But they don't. No magic number of flyers or YouTube videos or Facebook friends will change that.

Maybe that sounds like bad news. But here's the good news: if you focus your limited marketing resources on the people who really do matter most to your organization's success, you'll spend a lot less money and time, and you'll get better results. You'll actually make a difference.

Defining your audience has other benefits too, like minimizing office squabbling and handwringing. Once you define your audience and learn all you can about them, the answers to questions like "What should we put in the newsletter?" and "What color palette should we use on our website?" all become much easier to answer, because you'll know exactly who you are writing and designing them for.

RECOGNIZE THAT YOU HAVE MULTIPLE AUDIENCES

So just who are these people who matter most to your success? To define your audience, first you need to recognize that most nonprofits have multiple audiences. (I'm not crazy about the term "audience," by the way, because it suggests a one-way performance on your part. But lacking a better alternative, that's what we'll use.) Call them your target audiences, target populations, supporters, participants, clients, newsletter readers, website visitors—whatever you like.

Your next challenge is to segment those audiences into specific groups, held together by common characteristics or values. To do so, you'll need to define what ties the people in this group together, what they value, and how you can connect those values to your cause. You can further describe those groups by creating specific personas, which are typical characters within the group. As you define your audience by creating groups and personas, be aware of cultural stereotypes and of gatekeepers—people you need to go through to reach your intended target audience.

Because all nonprofits have multiple audiences, your marketing can sometimes go in divergent directions, just as the Jewish Council for Education and Research's did when it created TheGreatSchlep.com while also maintaining the much more mainstream JewsVote.org. You may need to think about how you communicate with clients or others who use your services; individual donors and volunteers; institutional funders like foundations, government grantmakers, and corporate sponsors; activists; partners; policymakers; and the media, to name a few.

At a minimum, most nonprofits have two audiences: the people they serve in some way and the people who support that mission financially. Sometimes these groups do overlap. A portion of your clientele or volunteers may also be donors. But other times the groups are very different. You may run a homeless shelter, but the people who donate to you may have never set foot in one. The more your audiences overlap, the less complicated your marketing strategy will be. But don't leap to that one-size-fits-all solution until you carefully analyze your audience by breaking them down into groups and personas.

SEGMENT YOUR TARGET AUDIENCE INTO GROUPS

You can use several techniques to break down the "general public" into more manageable and more meaningful groups.

Basic Demographics

Are most of your target audience men or women? How old are they? Do they live or work in certain places? Are most a particular ethnic group? Is income or education level relevant? Also consider factors that define how they spend their time. Where are they, and what are they doing there, from 9:00 AM to 5:00 PM or on weekends? What is their family status? Do they rent or own? Does this group of people tend to have strong likes or dislikes?

Behaviors

What is this group of people (perhaps independent of demographics) doing or not doing related to your cause? Think about your calls to action. Are they doing the right thing, but in the wrong place or at the wrong time? Social change comes about by individuals within a group changing their actions, so what kind of behavior changes would you like to see members of this group making?

The Stages of Change

If you are trying to convince people to modify their behaviors in significant ways (say, to quit smoking or to recycle more), the Stages of Change may be a helpful way to break down your target audience into smaller groups. The stages of change, known more formally as the transtheoretical model in health psychology, is often used in social marketing.

The first stage is precontemplation, in which the individual doesn't yet acknowledge that a problem exists. Next is contemplation, in which the individual acknowledges the problem but has plenty of reasons why they can't be addressed. Preparation comes next, in which the individual says, "Okay, I'll give it a try." This is also known as the testing phase. Next is the action phase, in which the individual is ready and makes the change. The final stage is maintenance and relapse prevention, in which the individual works to make the behavior a habit. Table 4.1 presents some examples. The questions and needs of someone in the contemplation stage are quite different than those of someone in the maintenance stage, which means your marketing approaches to those two groups would be quite different too.

EXAMPLE: DEFINING ONE SEGMENT OF A TARGET AUDIENCE

To illustrate this process, let's say we run a community center that operates a variety of different programs, including a family computer lab, after-school tutoring and recreation for teens, and meal delivery to homebound seniors. Our professional staff manages the programs, but we rely heavily on volunteers to implement the programs day to day. We are funded through a diverse mix of

Table 4.1.
The Stages of Change

Stage	Description	Typical State of Mind
Precontemplation	Does not recognize problem and has no intent to change	"Not my problem."
Contemplation	Recognizes problem; considering action	"I'll think about it."
Preparation	On the verge of taking action to make a change	"I need to do something. I'll give it a try."
Action	Making changes	"I'm ready. Let's do it."
Maintenance	Trying to maintain those changes	"I'm sticking with it."

government contracts, foundation grants, and donations from individuals and service organizations (for example, church group and civic club donations).

Rather than asking the "general public" to "support" our "programs"—three phrases so generic that they are essentially meaningless—we decide to break down our target audience into several groups. We start first with a behavior we are seeking: volunteering. We further refine this, using the stages of change, to people who are in either the contemplation or preparation stages. They know these needs exist in our community and that our nonprofit is working to address them, but they don't think volunteering is right for them for some reason, or they have considered volunteering but haven't actually contacted us yet.

We take it one step further by breaking down our group into four subgroups, defined by what we have historically understood to be the primary motivation for volunteering with our organization: retired people who want to stay active, people who are trying to build their résumés, people who want to give back to their communities, and people who want to change the world.

USE PERSONAS TO MORE CLEARLY DESCRIBE YOUR GROUPS

Breaking your target audience down into groups can feel impersonal. You add personality back into the process by creating personas within your groups.

Personas are good examples of individuals who are typical of the larger group. They are vivid descriptions of individual people, real or imaginary, who are members of the group. Be very specific as you describe each persona. Give each an age (not an age range), a name, income and educational levels, hobbies, and so on. Find a stock photo to represent each individual persona. You may create three or four personas per group.

Where do these three or four people come from? Start with your gut reaction. If you've been working in the field or for your organization for a while, you'll probably have a good sense for who the members of this group are. You can supplement your gut reaction by asking others who also work with the group for theirs and by observing the group in action.

Next, to build out this character, explore what each of these personas values most. You are no longer thinking about the general public. You aren't even thinking about the larger group or your cause. Instead, you are thinking about the values of these three or four individuals. What's important to them in their daily lives?

Here is a small sample of the kinds of values you might assign to your personas:

Time	Status	Cooperation	Pragmatism
Sleep	Power	Idealism	Privacy
Convenience	Fitting In	Safety	Connecting
Adventure	Change	Money	Independence
Public recognition	Self-Help	Efficiency	Teamwork
Good karma	Competition	Challenge	Predictability
Control	Action	Peace and quiet	Fun
Love	Formality	Compliance	Exclusivity
Openness	Learning	Spirituality	Exhilaration

EXAMPLE: CREATING SPECIFIC PERSONAS WITHIN A SEGMENTED GROUP

Now let's create four personas, one for each of the subgroups that we believe represent our most likely new volunteers. We'll describe them as specific people, whether real or imaginary.

Anna represents our retired person who wants to remain active. She is a sixty-seven-year-old Chinese-American. She and her husband Frank ran several small businesses in the community over the years and were very involved in the Chamber of Commerce and other civic groups, but since retiring a few years ago they have turned all of that over to their children and business partners. Anna is pursuing some new passions, including watercolors and tennis. Frank has cancer, and Anna is his primary caregiver.

What does Anna value? She values predictability and time, because she is pursuing other passions, but also taking care of her sick husband. She used to be a mover-and-shaker in the business community and misses some of that visibility, so she also values some public recognition.

Jessica represents our résumé builders. She is a thirty-two-year-old African-American single mother of two girls, ages five and eight. She works full-time as an administrative assistant, but the pay is hourly without good benefits. She would like to build her project management skills so that she can apply for executive assistant jobs that are salaried, with benefits. Her ex-husband is still in the girls' lives, but he travels for work so he is not a reliable source of childcare. As is true for most single parents, time, money and convenience are extremely valuable to Jessica. Self-help is essential to her long-term goals for her family, and spirituality is also a major part of her life.

John represents our volunteers who want to give back. He's your classic white male baby boomer who's living a comfortable upper-middle-class life with his wife, who is a homemaker and volunteer extraordinaire in her own right. His two kids are doing well in private colleges, and he looks forward to having grandchildren to bounce on his knees in a few years. He wears a suit and tie to work at the bank every day, but changes into a golf shirt and shorts as soon as he gets home. John feels lucky to have what he does, even though he believes he has earned it. He wants to give back, but on his own terms. He values efficiency and control.

Miguel represents our volunteers who want to change the world. He is an idealistic nineteen-year-old Latino who is fluent in both Spanish and English. His parents immigrated here when they were about Miguel's age and have told him many stories about the poverty they endured as children in their native countries. He is attending community college, because he isn't sure what he wants to do with his life yet, but he hopes to transfer to a four-year college the year after next. He has many interests, and they change often, so he's not likely to commit to anything long term. At the moment he's into hip-hop, baseball, and hanging out with his friends. Miguel values fun, fitting in, and making the world a better place.

AVOID CULTURAL STEREOTYPES

Creating groups and personas is by definition a form of stereotyping. There's no way around that. Your challenge is to ensure that you are describing characters who are truly representative of the group. Although they should be stereotypes of the people most important to the success of your organization, be sure that you are not inadvertently assigning characteristics that are false cultural stereotypes.

This is particularly dangerous when a nonprofit's staff have little direct experience with the specific type of persona they are creating. For example, I was working on creating a set of personas with a community-based health organization. One of the personas we were working on was a drug-abusing, low-income, African-American woman.

Several of the staff members had degrees in social work and public health, but had no direct experience working with low-income, female drug abusers. Their initial characterization was what someone in the room called a "crack whore"—a skinny woman with dirty clothes and hair, always looking for someone to sell her body to for the next fix.

Then another staff member spoke up. He had abused drugs himself at one point earlier in his life and had worked with this kind of persona often over the last several years. The picture he drew was quite different. The persona he described was someone who tried to look presentable at least most of the time so that she could hold down a part-time job and fly under the radar with people who would frown on her drug use—like her employers, family elders, and even her children. Although she would still trade sex for drugs, it wasn't something she did daily. After much discussion, the group decided that this persona was much closer to the organization's target audience than the one they had started with.

WATCH FOR GATEKEEPERS AND CREATE PERSONAS FOR THEM, TOO

In some cases, to reach your ultimate target audience, you may need to go through someone else first. Think of this person as the bouncer at a hot nightclub or the gatekeeper at the estate. They control who and what flows through to the other side, where your real target audience is. Analyzing the needs and interests of the gatekeepers can be just as important to your success as reaching your intended target audience. You may need to create separate personas for the gatekeepers too.

For example, if you run a sports program for children, you need to get the kids excited about playing so you'll describe the activities in ways that emphasize fun, friends, and competition. But you also need to convince the parents to enroll their children in the program and pay the fee. Although the parents also want their kids to have fun, they are more likely to be concerned about you providing a safe learning environment, and your marketing materials should address those interests and concerns.

If you want to reach out to twenty-somethings about preventing sexually transmitted infections, you may literally run into bouncers. One of the most effective ways to deliver your message is to go where your target audience already is, especially when they are making decisions related to your issue. Therefore, if you wanted to reach people who may be considering having unprotected sex with each other, your job will be easier if you develop cooperative partnerships with club owners and bar managers. To convince those people to allow you to put beer coasters with safe sex messages on the bar and a condom display in the bathroom, you first have to address their concerns about hassling their customers and interfering with their sales.

The gatekeepers aren't always obvious. In the 1990s, Atlanta officials wanted to prevent holiday outbreaks of diarrhea cases in infants, which they associated with the preparation of chitterlings (or "chitlins"—pig intestines) by African-American women.[1] For several years, health officials passed out flyers through WIC clinics to mothers of infants, emphasizing hand washing and keeping kids away from the raw chitterlings. They were treating the mothers like the gatekeepers for the infants.

But the outbreaks continued. In 1996, after some target audience research, they tried a new approach that was directed at the real gatekeepers: grandmothers who actually did the shopping and cooking around the holidays, passed on the traditions, and also cared for the infants. Secondary audiences were pastors, church leaders, and grocery store managers. They also changed the messaging to address a very common myth among family matriarchs that preboiling the chitterlings, as the health department suggested, would "boil in the dirt" and ruin the taste. The right message, sent through the right gatekeeper, worked, and the cases of infant diarrhea declined dramatically.

CONCLUSION: DON'T JUMP AHEAD TO TACTICS

In the rush to get everything done, many nonprofits jump straight to tactics without first considering who the target audiences for those tactics are. If you find yourself struggling with tactical questions, go back to square one: who are we trying to communicate with and what do they care about?

You will inevitably have multiples audiences with different values, needs, and interests. But if you work through the process of defining both your groups and your personas, you will be able to see the points where your communications to each of them can overlap into one multi-audience strategy and where you will likely need to create separate, specialized strategies. Each audience, for example, may receive the same message, but packaged in a different communications tactic (for example, you reach one group through mainstream media publicity; you reach the other primarily through word-of-mouth messages spread through faith communities). Or each audience group may get its own message through its own communications channels, yet those separate messages work together well to create progress toward your mission (for example, doctors get one message at their offices about talking to their patients about cancer prevention; patients get a different message at home about talking to their doctors about cancer prevention).

Understanding your target audience is the first step in creating both strategies and tactics that will work.

chapter
FIVE

Create a Powerful Message: What Do You Want to Say?

If I look at the mass I will never act. If I look at the one, I will.

—Mother Teresa

This chapter is about . . .

- Several characteristics of powerful messages
- Creating messages that appeal to your target audience's values
- Making the "benefit exchange" between you and your audience clear

How do you get members of your target audience to help you with the big problems you are trying to solve? You have to make it personal and meaningful to them. In Chapter Four, we looked at ways to leave behind the notion of the general public and to instead look at the groups and personas who are most important to your nonprofit's success. Now it's time to craft messages that connect personally with those members of your target audience.

The most powerful messages used by nonprofits embody at least one of these characteristics:

- They emphasize the impact on one person, animal, or thing
- They evoke specific emotions
- They reinforce personal identity
- They validate a decision or action by appealing to reason
- They have a clear, strong call to action

THE POWER OF ONE OVER MANY

On May 10, 2007, *New York Times* op-ed columnist Nicholas Kristof wrote a column called "Save the Darfur Puppy."[1] He lamented that publicizing the suffering of a puppy with big eyes and floppy ears would do what the suffering of hundreds of thousands could not: motivate the world's leaders to end the genocide in Sudan. Many experienced fundraisers thought to themselves, "You know, he's right."

The psychological research that Kristof quoted in his column backs up what veteran fundraising copywriters know too: asking someone to help one person (or one puppy) is likely to produce more action than asking that person to help thousands of people.

Research by Paul Slovic of Decision Research and the University of Oregon shows that people who are otherwise caring and would go out of their way to help another individual become numb and indifferent to the suffering of the masses.[2] In one experiment, people were given $5 to donate to alleviate hunger overseas. The first choice was to give the money to a particular child, Rokia, a seven-year-old in Mali. The second choice was to help twenty-one million hungry Africans. The third choice was to help Rokia, but as just one of many victims of hunger. Can you guess which choice was most popular?

Slovic reported that donations to the individual, Rokia, were far greater than donations to the second choice, the statistical portrayal of the hunger crisis. That's not particularly surprising. But what is surprising, and some would say discouraging, is that adding the statistical realities of the larger hunger problem to Rokia's story significantly reduced the contributions to Rokia. Giving the donor the larger perspective didn't work.

A follow-up study allowed donors to give to Rokia or to a hungry boy named Moussa. Both Rokia and Moussa attracted similar levels of donations. But when given the option of donating to both Rokia and Moussa together, contributions fell off 15 percent. In another experiment, donors who were shown a photo of eight starving children contributed 50 percent less money than those who were shown a photo of a single child.

We are more compelled to act when we feel a direct connection with one person or one living creature we can help. You may recall the starfish story. On a beach where thousands of starfish have been stranded, an old man is throwing them back into the ocean. A young man walking by tells the old man, "You can't possibly make a difference." As another starfish lands safely back in the sea, the old man replies, "It makes a difference to that one." And he keeps picking them up and saving them, one by one.

The motivating power of focusing on just one works in many ways in nonprofit marketing. You need to speak to each of your supporters as individuals. You need to speak about the impact of their donations on other individuals. And you need to speak as an individual working on this cause, rather than as the monolithic nonprofit organization. Good nonprofit marketing is about creating and building the relationships between these individuals, as well as the network or community of support you create when you add all of these relationships together.

THE POWER OF EMOTIONAL CONTENT

If you ask veterans of hard-fought political campaigns which matters most—what a person *feels* or what a person *thinks* about your candidate—they will tell you, without exception, that heart overrules head in the voting booth.[3] The same goes for the way we make purchasing decisions, the way people vote on juries, and whether we support charitable causes.

As described in *Brand Immortality: How Brands Can Live Long and Prosper* by Hamish Pringle and Peter Field, the U.K.-based Institute of Practitioners in Advertising analyzed 1,400 case studies of successful advertising. They compared the profitability boost of ads that appealed primarily to emotions versus those that relied on rational information like statistics. Ad campaigns with purely emotional content outperformed the rational-only content by two to one. Ads that were purely emotional also performed better than ads with mixed emotional and rational content, though by a much smaller margin.

These results affirm what Dr. Robert Heath of the University of Bath's School of Management found in 2006. He found that U.S. and U.K. television advertisements with high levels of emotional content made the advertising successful, not the message itself. The emotional ads enhanced how people felt about brands being advertised. Ads with low levels of emotion had no effect, even when they were factual and informative.

We want to *feel* good about what we are doing, so we make decision with our hearts (or guts) and then analyze selective facts in our heads to justify those decisions. But which emotions motivate us the most? Best-selling author and marketer Seth Godin says the three most important emotions in marketing are fear, hope, and love.

Many studies, especially in the social marketing community, have shown that fear can motivate people to change their behaviors, but only when it's very clear that the threat to themselves or loved ones is real. Ways to avert the threat must also be clear and doable. Otherwise people are likely to be both defensive and dismissive of your message.

Although fear-based messaging is usually used in a negative way—"This bad thing will happen if you don't take this action"—you can also accept fear as one of the characteristics of your target audience and then offer them positive ways to overcome that fear.

That's the approach that the staff of Alberta Health Services in Medicine Hat, Alberta, took when trying to increase the number of women getting screened for cervical cancer. The staff met with groups of women in the target audience in informal focus groups and listened to their fears, which included that the screening would produce a positive result for cancer and that unskilled health providers with clumsy hands would be performing the Pap tests.

Based on what they heard, the staff redrafted the clinic's marketing messages, which are now about freeing women from those fears. One key message is ". . . because I want to know that everything is okay." Images emphasize the comfort of dealing with skilled and qualified health professionals.

"We recognize the concept of fear and immediately get beyond that point in the minds of our audience," says Gordon Wright, a health promotions facilitator. "The negative is quickly introduced as a concept, and we deal with it from a positive point of view, getting beyond the issue immediately." Within five months, the staff turned a stale direct mail campaign into one that has motivated so many women that appointment slots are booked six weeks in advance.

So what about the power of love and hope? The message of hope and possibility certainly worked for Barack Obama's 2008 presidential campaign, and most fundraising experts will tell you that's what they prefer too, if you are in it for the long run. Although messages that induce fear may work in the short run, donors will quickly tire of your "the sky is falling" tactics.

Direct mail fundraising expert Mal Warwick, author of *How to Write Successful Fundraising Letters*, is a strong believer in hopeful versus fearful or angry messaging in fundraising. Although fear-mongering can and has worked, especially in the political arena, says Mal, when you don't have anything constructive to say and can't articulate a vision, anger and fear soon grow old. "Those hit pieces mailed into voters' homes shortly before elections by unscrupulous candidates and consultants have the principal effect of depressing voter turnout," says Mal. "In other words, as a motivator, negative messaging falls flat."

Donors expect more of the nonprofit community. "They may well respond impulsively with a first-time gift to an appeal that's blatantly based on fear, anger, greed, or guilt, but they're much less likely to keep giving unless they learn about some more constructive aspect of an organization's work," says Mal.

Jeff Brooks, author of the "Future Fundraising Now" blog (one of my favorites), also believes that positive messages outperform negative ones. One of his nonprofit clients that works on cancer research tried two different messages: a scary one that emphasized the likelihood of the recipient or someone they loved getting cancer versus a more hopeful one emphasizing how cancer treatments are making the illness more survivable every day. The more positive message is raising more money than the negative one.

At the same time, Jeff reports that fundraising appeals that include matching funds and other leverage-your-giving offers do very well in almost every context. With these kinds of appeals, it works best, says Jeff, to focus on the increased impact of the donor's giving, not on the depth of the problem the donor is solving. Again, focusing on positive results works better than emphasizing a negative situation.

THE POWER OF PERSONAL IDENTITY

How supporters feel about themselves in relation to your cause, as well as the stereotypes associated with your cause and your messaging, will also affect how likely they are to support you. Several studies have shown, for example, that when Asian girls are asked to identify their gender on a math test, they don't do as well (because of the stereotype that girls aren't good at math). But when they are asked to identify their ethnicity, they do much better (because of the stereotype that Asians are good at math). The role of personal identity in how we make decisions and behave is another important factor for you to consider as you develop messages for your target audiences.

Can you tap into the personal identity of a segment of your supporters and use a link to your organization to affirm that identity? Describe what it is like to be in their shoes, then see if you can find a natural connection to your organization. "I am a [describe the person's identity] and therefore supporting this cause feels entirely natural to me because [explain how it reinforces the person's identity]."

I have given to my alma mater, the University of California at Berkeley, one time and one time only. Since I graduated way back in 1991, I've received countless letters highlighting the academic achievements of some very smart, usually much older than me, scientists and engineers on the campus. Problem is, I don't understand half of what they are talking about. Although I'm a fairly analytical person, I despised physics, and my only C at Cal was in astronomy.

But in the fall of 2007, I received a direct mail piece from Cal that blew me away.[4] On the cover, it asked, "Who are you? Cal alumni are . . ." The "you" was in big, bright yellow letters, standing out against a black background. As I opened the piece and unfolded it, I saw a series of panels:

- Movement Leaders & Story Weavers
- Creators & Innovators
- Educators & Crusaders
- Trendsetters & Friend Seekers
- Activists & Satirists

Each tag included a clear, simple image with a small blurb about an alum who exemplifies that description. On the Movement Leaders panel, I saw a bunch of asparagus, and "Alice Waters, '67. Acclaimed chef and pioneer behind the worldwide movement to eat local, organic foods." On the Friend Seekers panel, I saw a screenshot of Tom's MySpace page with 201,904,463 friends. It read, "Tom Anderson, '98. Cofounder and president of MySpace.com and first friend to every user."

The ten images represent a great diversity in alumni in age, gender, ethnicity, and subject area. They are chefs, writers, teachers, scientists, programmers, inventers, cartoonists, and athletes who all have had a profound impact on today's culture. Real people, cool people.

On the donation form and envelope, the appeal closes with these simple phrases that say it all to the alumni would-be donors: "Cal alumni are changing the world. Won't YOU champion the next generation of innovators?" followed by "Thanks for being who you are. We appreciate your generosity."

With the fundraising letters I had received before, my internal dialogue went something like, "Sheesh, these old guys are really smart. I don't understand what they are talking about. Did I actually graduate from Cal?" With this new piece, the internal dialogue went like this: "Wow, I went to the same school as these creative, independent firebrands. I'm one of them. I want to support Cal because it nurtures and graduates innovative, free-thinking people like me." I got out my credit card and made a $50 donation.

THE POWER OF LOGIC, REASON, AND STATISTICS

If you stopped reading this chapter now, you might believe that there is no room for reason or statistics in your nonprofit marketing. But you'd be wrong. Remember, most people make decisions based on emotion, then rationalize or justify those decisions with reason. People decide which charities to support based on an emotional response to the cause, but if you ask them later to explain why they chose that charity, they will often rattle off a list of logical, fact-based reasons. This isn't unique to philanthropy—this basic process of emotion driving decision making and reason justifying those emotions happens in all aspects of our lives. This means that there's definitely a role for statistics in your marketing, but you have to be smart about how you use them. You want facts and statistics to be easily understood and memorable, so that your supporters can recall them later, when explaining to friends and family why they are so generous to your cause.

People have a hard time understanding really big numbers, whether you are talking about millions of people, miles, or hours. The difference between four thousand people dying and forty thousand people dying is hard for the brain to comprehend. It's just a whole lot of people dying. If the number is overwhelming, then so is the situation, which makes your supporters turn away. They won't be moved by the big number, nor will they remember it, unless you provide some kind of context to make the number real to them.

The Frameworks Institute, which looks at various ways to frame the way we talk about social issues, suggests that nonprofits too often use really big numbers to emphasize the magnitude of a problem or crisis and then end up using small numbers when talking about solutions, leaving supporters with a sense of futility.[5] They recommend using "social math" instead, which blends numbers into stories using analogies. Instead of talking about six tons of toxins being emitted into the air each day, for example, talk about twenty-five balloons full of toxic pollutants for each school child in town.

Do be careful about the analogies you use. Just because you make the number smaller doesn't mean it will be any easier to understand. The social math needs to make sense in the context of your target audience's day-to-day lives. It's also easy to lose sight of the original data once you turn statistics into stories. When you use social math, make sure you can always go back to the original numbers.

DOG PARKS: WHO CARES DURING A RECESSION?

I recall serving as a guest expert in an online chat about nonprofit marketing hosted by the *Chronicle of Philanthropy*. A community organization that was trying to start a dog park wanted to know how it could create compelling messages that would grab prospective supporters when it was competing against so many other causes that are much more directly related to desperate human needs, particularly during a recession.

My advice was to stop trying to compete directly on the basis of need, because it would be a losing battle. Instead, I encouraged the dog park advocates to look at other cultural trends and hot topics that people are captivated by right now and use those to make their messages meaningful. Take the cultural shift that's running parallel to the recession: people focusing more on what's really important to them and what brings about genuine quality of life. It's all about family and friends now, and dogs are both family *and* friends. I encouraged them to talk about the comfort and security that dogs give both kids and seniors. To step it up a notch, I suggested they try to find families of soldiers on deployment with kids and dogs left behind, or to find neighbors keeping dogs for soldiers at war, because the impact

of the wars in Iraq and Afghanistan on military families is also a hot topic with the media.

Connecting your cause to societal trends and media headlines is a powerful way to tweak your message so it gets more attention.

THE POWER OF A CLEAR CALL TO ACTION

Most of the content you create should end with some kind of call to action or next step. What do you want your readers to do next, now that they've read your newsletter? Surely not just delete it or recycle it and move on with their day? Calls to action can be very forceful and direct (for example, volunteer today, donate now, register) or more suggestive and lighter in tone (for example, learn more, tell a friend).

Include specific calls to action (and links in email and on web pages) that make following through as simple as possible. Make it what Katya Andresen, author of *Robin Hood Marketing: Stealing Corporate Savvy to Sell Just Causes*, calls a "filmable moment." Could you film your supporters following through on your call to action? If it is clear and simple enough, your supporters should be able to easily visualize themselves and others doing it.

The more time or money you request—the bigger investment you are asking someone to make in you—the more specific your call to action should be. Don't ask people to donate to your cause in the abstract. Explain where the money is going or how the volunteer's time will be used. If a donation is paying for salaries or overhead, talk about what those people actually do with their time and what results from that. What will be accomplished with my donation? That's what your supporters want to know.

CREATE MESSAGES THAT APPEAL TO YOUR TARGET AUDIENCE

Which of these elements should you incorporate into your message for your specific campaign? It all depends on your audience and what you think is most likely to move them. At this stage, it sometimes helps to think of your target audience as incredibly selfish people. Of course, the opposite is true. Many of your supporters are extremely generous human beings. But when creating messages about your programs, services, or campaigns, you have to make it all about them—your target audience. Appeal not to *your* needs or even the needs of the people you serve, but to the values and needs of your audience groups and personas. Make it worth their time.

In nonprofit marketing and especially in fundraising, that means acknowledging the need of your supporters to feel like they are personally making a genuine difference in the life of someone else when they contribute time, money, or influence to your cause. You have to get beyond the indifference to the masses that people naturally feel when confronted with famine or thousands of stranded starfish. Instead, empower them, through your messaging, to be the old man who is willing to make a difference for those starfish, one by one, by appealing to whatever their particular interests and values may be.

Once you have identified your target audience and you know who you need to talk to, how do you decide what to say to them? You need to find the intersection between what you want your audience to know and do with what they really care about, which may or may not be directly related to your cause.

You do that by describing your program and your call to action in ways that appeal to their values. In commercial marketing terms, you are converting the features of your product into benefits. Seatbelts and airbags in a car are safety features. Not dying in a car accident is a benefit. Red paint and shiny chrome on a sports car are features; feeling powerful and desirable as you drive that car are the benefits.

For nonprofits, converting the features of your good cause into benefits for your supporters often means looking for the emotional payback that your supporters get for giving time or money to your organization or for following through on whatever action you are asking them to take. It's called the benefit exchange. What's in it for them? Do the members of your target audience, after absorbing your message and following through on whatever call to action you've requested, get to feel effective, appreciated, powerful, included, heard, validated, relieved, or some other highly valued emotion?

Let's look at another example from the world of health marketing: teens and smoking. For many years, we told teens that they would die young if they smoked. Although the idea of dying young may seem tragic to the middle-aged people creating the campaign, it doesn't work with teenagers, who have little sense of their own mortality. In fact, dying young is often seen as romantic and tragically hip. Take another frequently used message, "Smoking hurts people around you." What's the typical teen reaction? "If everyone else around me is smoking, why should I care? It doesn't look like anyone is getting hurt; in fact, they seem to be having a pretty good time to me." The benefits of not smoking in these messages are a complete mismatch with teen values and are therefore not a benefit at all.

This kind of marketing to teens failed miserably, and teen smoking rates continued to rise. In 1998, the state of Florida decided to take a different approach and launched the "truth" campaign.[6] It was so successful that is has been adopted nationally by the American Legacy Foundation, which was formed to manage the funds from the 1998 Tobacco Master Settlement Agreement between tobacco companies and forty-six U.S. states. Instead of focusing on health concerns that are irrelevant to teens, the truth campaign focuses on the values that teens naturally embrace: rebelling against authority and assuming that adults are lying to them.

The truth campaign set up the tobacco company executives as the authority figures and portrayed them as evil adults who thought they could manipulate and trick teens into smoking. Now, instead of starting to smoke as a way to rebel, teens are refusing to smoke as a way to rebel! Here's how the American Legacy Foundation positions the truth message: "We're not anti-smoker, or anti-smoking. We're just anti-manipulations. With that in mind, we try to 'out' Big Tobacco's tactics so everyone knows what they're up to." It works, because it reinforces what teens are already feeling about the world around them.

You can do the same for your cause. Figure out what your target audience values, then create messages that either reinforce those values or remove barriers to reaching them.

EXAMPLE: MATCHING MESSAGES TO PERSONAS' VALUES

Let's go back to our community center example, in which we are trying to market our organization to new volunteers. How can we create messages that match the values of the four personas we created: Anna, Jessica, John, and Miguel?

Anna is our retired person who values predictability. She'd prefer specific, recurring tasks that can be accomplished in a set amount of time. She wants to come in, know what she's doing, get it done, and come back the same time next week. Our messaging to her should make clear that these kinds of set volunteer opportunities are available. She also wants to feel appreciated, so personal thank-you notes from organizational leaders as well as from the people the program helps will work well for her.

For our single mom, Jessica, convenient résumé-building opportunities are going to be most attractive. We need to market to her volunteer tasks that are going to let her stretch herself some, but that also offer some flexibility because of her busy schedule. Wouldn't it be great if we offered something fun for her kids to do while she volunteered? We need to show her that she can improve the lives of others while growing as a professional and as a provider for her family too.

For our baby boomer businessman, John, we'll be more successful if we emphasize that we have many choices for him and he has control over his volunteer experience. We also want to emphasize how his talents are going to produce real results within the community, so we'll back up the options we provide with data on the results he can expect. He'll enjoy meeting the people who benefit from his volunteer time.

Our college student Miguel will be more interested in short-term group activities where friends can volunteer together. We might incorporate a social aspect as well, such as buying pizza for volunteers after the center closes for the day. We might create a Facebook group where the teens could organize and plan their volunteer activities themselves.

Even though all four of these volunteers may end up performing similar tasks in our community center, these four personas want very different things out of the experience. If our marketing understands and reflects that, we'll be more successful in recruiting them and ultimately more successful in implementing our mission. Making sure that volunteers understand the real impact that they are having on the lives of specific individuals at the community center would round out marketing to these people.

Now let's say that after looking at our list of long-time donors, we realize that a significant percentage of them volunteered for us at some point. Therefore, we want to create a marketing plan that uses the same four personas we developed for our volunteers group, but now we'll look at ways to motivate them to donate money instead of time. How will their values affect our fundraising messages?

Anna is a retired business owner and is accustomed to public recognition. Leaving a legacy is important to her. That tells us that she might be interested in a planned giving option, such as including the community center in her estate plans. She may also be interested in some naming opportunities, whereby we will put her and her husband's names on an item in the center or name a program after them.

Our single mom, Jessica, has two small children and is unlikely to be interested in talking about estate planning with us. She might, however, be willing to consider a small monthly gift, so explaining the convenience of a monthly automated credit card charge or checking account deduction could work. She's also likely to be a good candidate for active fundraising events, particularly those she could do with her children, like a walk-a-thon. We could also encourage her to ask her church or other service clubs to raise money for the center.

Baby boomer John likes to have control over his philanthropy, so being clear that he can decide exactly which programs to fund will be important. We also need to ensure that we report back clearly and regularly on the successes that his generous giving produces at the center.

For our young idealist, Miguel, giving money at all may be difficult, so we need to make it easy. Fun events like dance-a-thons could work, and monthly giving at a modest level, even just $5 per month, could work too, as could donating occasionally through his mobile phone via a mobile giving campaign that adds the donation to his phone bill.

CONCLUSION: EVEN THE RELIEF WORKERS WANT TO SAVE THE DARFUR PUPPY

Shortly after Nicholas Kristof's column about the Darfur puppy was published, he received an email from an American relief worker who had actually saved a Darfur puppy.[7] The aid worker admitted to feeling "slightly ridiculous" about sneaking the weeks-old puppy onto a plane to Khartoum and eventually back to the United States. The Sudan-born dog now lives a happy American life, complete with dog walker, naps on the couch, and romps through the park. Here's how the aid worker described the aftermath of this decision to Kristof:

> I also felt guilty, and still do, that I did so much to save a puppy from Darfur, but not enough to save its people. In that sense, I'm afraid I have a classic case of "psychic numbing," especially after living in Sudan. My only feeble defense is the immediacy of my action—the instant satisfaction I received from saving a life (even a dog's), and the joy I have from watching her grow up.

Even someone who more completely understands the suffering of thousands is still moved by power of saving one.

chapter
six

Deliver Your Message: How and Where Are You Going to Say It?

The more elaborate our means of communication,
the less we communicate.

—Joseph Priestley

This chapter is about . . .

- Packaging your message into words and images
- Choosing the best communications channels
- Increasing the likelihood that your audience will get your message

You've defined your audience and created a powerful message that will appeal to them and move them to follow through on your call to action. Now how do you deliver that message to your audience? You'll need to package it in words and images that will travel to your audiences' eyes and ears. You'll likely use multiple communications channels, both in print and online, to accomplish this, searching for ways to reach your audience where they already are.

PACKAGE YOUR MESSAGE INTO WORDS

Straight "just the facts" reporting of your messages and supporting information can work in some cases, but your messaging will often be more effective if you use either an "empowering tips" or narrative storytelling approach.

Empowering tips show your supporters how they can make decisions and take actions in their own lives in a way that contributes to your overall mission. Tips can come in many formats, such as how-to articles, advice columns, top ten lists, and reviews. You can provide talking points that your supporters can use when chatting with their friends, family, and peers about your issues. Though these articles or video/audio scripts will often be straightforward and objective, by putting them into a helpful format you can more easily connect your message with your audience's needs and values.

Narrative storytelling allows you to use more emotion in sharing your message. You share someone's story, and by hearing or seeing that story your audiences learn valuable lessons from it or are inspired to take some kind of action. You can teach by example by telling success stories, profiling interesting people, taking supporters behind the scenes, and letting your clients or supporters tell their own stories in their own words through first-person testimonials. You can also share lessons learned by explaining how you goofed something up, what you learned, and what you are doing differently now.

Whether you take the empowering tips or narrative storytelling approach, your writing style and word choices should support that approach. Most often, you'll want to strive for a friendly, conversational tone. This is especially true when writing fundraising text; here your goal is to create a long-term relationship with the donor.

UCLA and USC researchers have found that narrative text (for example, descriptive storytelling), as opposed to expository writing (for example, straight reporting), creates powerful neural responses in the brain. This, says Frank Dickenson of Claremont Graduate University, explains why it's hard to put down a novel but easy to fall asleep reading a textbook (but not this one, of course!).

In his 2009 doctoral research study "The Way We Write Is All Wrong," Dickenson put 1.5 million words of fundraising text from both direct mail and websites of 880 nonprofits through what he calls a "linguistic MRI." Unfortunately, what he found is that fundraising text actually focuses much more on transferring information than on storytelling, and it contains far less narrative than both academic prose and official documents. Fundraising text also lacks linguistic features that create emotional connections with readers, such as personal verbs like *I feel* and *I think*, contractions, past-tense verbs, and quoted speech.

Don't bury your well-focused and targeted message in jargon and other stiff language that doesn't connect with your audience. Spend time finding the right words that package your message in a way that your audience will find attractive and compelling.

SUPPORT YOUR WORDS WITH IMAGES

Photography and graphics—both stills and video—can be incredibly powerful in conveying your message. You can use actual images of your organization's activities to show exactly what it is you do and who's doing it for whom. You can visually show problems and solutions. You can also use symbolic imagery to reinforce metaphors you may be using to get your points across (for example, a photo of a seedling to convey early growth or a large old tree to convey enduring strength).

It's best to use your own original photos and video, but when you don't have the right images for your message, consider using stock photography. It's true that many people despise stock photography because much of it looks too polished, posed, generic, or fake. But if you are clear about the type of image you want or the metaphor you are trying to illustrate, a few minutes searching through one of the major stock photography websites will often be fruitful. Stock images can cost as little as a $1 for a web-quality image and from $10 to several hundred for a print quality image. My favorite stock image site for affordable photos is istockphoto.com. They have the best search engine, which makes it much easier to find the right photo fast. See the companion website for more recommendations on where to find affordable stock photography.

For an alternative to stock photography sites, try photo-sharing sites like Flickr.com where both professional and amateur photographers upload and share their photographs. Although it is often harder to find the right image on photo-sharing sites because the images typically aren't tagged and catalogued as thoroughly as they are on stock photography sites, you will usually find much more natural, "real life" photography. Photo-sharing sites will often be your best option if you need something gritty, funny, a little strange, or offbeat.

Regardless of where you find the image, you must always be aware of the copyrights attached to it, which determine what anyone other than the original creator can and cannot do with the image and under what terms. When you purchase photos from a stock photography site, you will be given options for the types of rights you want to purchase. On photo-sharing sites, you should look carefully to see what rights the photographer is offering.

One popular rights management program is Creative Commons, which allows creators of content, including photography, to specify the conditions under which others may use their photos at no cost. For example, under the Creative Commons "By" license, you can use a photo without paying the photographer as long as you give credit to that photographer wherever you use the photo. Other licenses limit the use of photos to noncommercial purposes and the extent to which a photo can be modified. Flickr allows you to search by the type of license you want.

Get in the habit of taking photos all the time (a great job for a volunteer), use stock photography or photo-sharing sites to fill in the gaps, and use photography in all of your communications offline and online.

SELECT THE BEST COMMUNICATIONS CHANNELS FOR YOUR AUDIENCE

You have your text and images. Now let's take a quick look at some of the most popular communications channels used by nonprofits today. Your marketing program will be most effective when you use multiple channels to get your message across and to promote conversations with your supporters. (In many cases, you'll end up selecting the channel first, then developing the text and images for that channel. It doesn't matter so much which comes first, as long as the result accomplishes the goal of delivering your messages to your target audiences.)

Newsletter. The default communications channel to supporters for most nonprofits is a newsletter, whether in print or email or both. Many nonprofits send quarterly newsletters, but if that's all you are sending, that's usually not enough to get your messages to stick. I believe it's better to produce a one- or two-page print newsletter or five-hundred-word e-newsletter once a month than it is to produce an eight-page print newsletter once a quarter.

Other direct mail. From appeal letters and thank-you notes to event invitations and postcards, print mail (or snail mail) has always been central to nonprofit marketing. Many organizations are rightly reevaluating how much direct mail they send now and in what format because of cost considerations. Your organization needs to find the right mix of print and online communications, given your audience, your messaging, and your own communications capabilities.

Website. Every nonprofit needs a basic website. Your website is your online home base; if you don't have one, your credibility immediately drops. Having a decent website is a sign of professionalism.

Social networking. Social media—including social networking sites like Facebook, LinkedIn, Twitter, and MySpace—have changed the way that people connect and stay in touch. If you think it's just for young people, it's time to wake up and ask around. You'll be surprised how many people in their forties, fifties, and sixties are using these sites daily—so many in fact that teenagers are saying Facebook and Twitter are no longer cool. (But keep in mind, unless teenagers are one of your target audiences, what they think doesn't really matter to your organization. What matters is whether your target audience is using these sites.)

Case studies, white papers, and reports. Publish your own reports and e-books as PDFs and offer them as free downloads on your website. You can sell them online, too.

Video and podcasts. It's easier and cheaper than ever to produce web-quality video and audio (podcasts). It's so much easier to share the human side of your work and the personality of your organization when people can hear your voice and see your face. Many people also prefer to get information by watching or listening rather than reading.

Photos and slide decks. Even if you don't have the audio to go along with them, photo essays and slide presentations can quickly convey information through the power of imagery, juxtaposed with a few words in the form of photo captions or slideshow text.

Advertising. Nonprofits are using print, TV, radio, and online advertising, particularly search advertising like Google Adwords, to promote their issues and organizations. Online advertising coupled with well-designed and inspiring landing pages can persuade people searching for information on various topics to become email newsletters subscribers and online donors.

Telephone calls. Although few people will admit to liking telemarketing, it can be effective when used in very specific ways (for example, university students calling alumni, meeting reminders or urgent announcements sent by robocall to discrete, opt-in groups like club members).

Texting. The number of mobile phones worldwide has surpassed landlines, and some demographic groups on the other side of the digital divide, including some low-income and minority populations, are connecting to the Internet primarily through mobile devices.

Events. Whether it's in-person or online, getting everyone together for a fun or educational event remains a tried-and-true method to reach your target audiences. Events include workshops, webinars, parties, meet-ups, briefings, Internet radio shows, work camps, celebrations, and more.

Publicity. Getting media coverage of your organization and its work can bring your story to potential new supporters, whether it appears in print, online, on TV, or on the radio. Many practitioners now broaden this beyond mainstream media to include anyone creating content that could sway public opinion, such as bloggers or even individuals using Facebook or Twitter to spread messages to their friends.

Personal Visits. Nothing beats the personal touch. Whether negotiating a case management plan for a client or a major gift, in-person meetings are best for convincing others to do something for us or with us.

Word-of-Mouth. The younger you are, the more likely you are to trust what your friends say over any other way of receiving information. Even middle-aged people are jaded by advertising and overloaded by information. What we hear from people we trust matters, making word-of-mouth marketing extremely important to nonprofits (and it's cheap!).

COMMUNITY THEATER USES SOCIAL MEDIA GAME TO LURE VISITORS TO CAFÉ

The Marsh, a community theater in San Francisco, operates a café that doubles as a box office and lobby for performances. But in early 2009 no one was patronizing the café, and it was losing money. "Our theater billed itself as a 'breeding ground for new performance,' and yet that brand didn't extend to our café, which should have appeared equally hip and innovative," explains operations manager Cari Turley. "But it didn't."

In addition to practical steps like improving the menu, extending the hours, and remodeling, The Marsh created an innovative promotion with the social media game Foursquare.com. The game lets you check in to various locations with your cell phone, and it tells all of your friends who are also playing the game where you are. You can also publish your check-ins to your Twitter and Facebook accounts. The game includes many incentives for checking in, like "mayorship" for the person who checks in the most and

badges for certain patterns of behavior. You can also leave tips for future travelers in various locations.

The Marsh put a sign in its window, saying that the Foursquare Mayor would drink for free at the café, and that anyone (mayor and non-mayor alike) who checked in would get $2 off a ticket to any show playing that night. The café is also the box office, after all. The Marsh was the first café in San Francisco to use the game, and the story was picked up by some major blogs, including TechCrunch. "Suddenly we weren't toiling in obscurity anymore," says Cari.

Within a few weeks, new menu items were flying off the shelves. "We were no longer seen as that 'abandoned warehouse–looking building,' as one blogger put it," says Cari. "Public perception of our brand became a lot closer to our perception, and we started to see increased audience numbers—and coffee drinkers—because of it."

USE MULTIPLE CHANNELS TO REINFORCE YOUR MESSAGE

Although some kind of newsletter is the default starting point for a nonprofit communications program, your newsletter shouldn't be your only means of communication. It's best to connect with your supporters through multiple channels. You can reinforce a message you sent via a postcard with an email. You can remind people about an event you marketed primarily through email by messaging the fans of your Facebook page or posting a reminder on your blog. Although you should publish an annual report at the end of your fiscal year, you should also be reporting on successes throughout the year in your newsletters and through social media. Reaching your supporters with the same message through multiple channels greatly increases the odds of them actually paying attention to it.

As much as possible, make your communications channels two-way, and let your audience reply to you through multiple channels. Some will prefer to call you during office hours and others will prefer to send you an email or a message on Facebook in the evening. By using several communications channels, you give your supporters more options for communicating their opinions and ideas back to you.

One common concern about using multiple channels is the fear of repetition. But remember, repetition has its benefits in marketing. The conventional wisdom is that a person has to hear or see a message somewhere between three and seven times before it sinks in. But your supporters are not reading every single thing you send them. Even if they technically receive the same message in three different places, they may actually read or hear it in only one of those places, overlooking it in the other two. And people are not committing what they do read to memory, which means you need to deliver your message even more often—perhaps as many as twenty times before it really gets through.

At the same time, when people are connecting with you in multiple channels, you don't want to bore or annoy them with too much duplication. You can easily avoid that by simply remixing your content as part of a content creation strategy. While keeping your message consistent, you can use different words, visuals, formats, and channels to get that message across, so it feels fresh to your supporters but still reinforces a consistent message.

One downside of using multiple channels is that it makes it harder to measure the effectiveness of any one particular channel. Although you may be able to connect a certain level of fundraising income to a particular direct mail letter, for example, those donors may have been much more inclined to give because they received your email newsletter monthly throughout the year. Therefore the newsletter is contributing to the success of the direct mail campaign. Difficulty in measuring the impact of your specific communications channels is a minor downside compared to the overwhelming benefits of reaching out to your supporters in multiple ways.

PUT YOUR MESSAGE WHERE YOUR AUDIENCE IS ALREADY GOING

One of the easiest ways to select the right channels is to think about where your target audience is already going and to take your message to them there. Where do these people get their news? Do they read the paper, watch TV, listen to the radio, or spend most of their day online? Are particular groups of friends, family, or coworkers influential? Do they attend regular church services, or soccer practices, or Chamber of Commerce meetings? Where do they go during the day and at night? Where do they work, shop, and relax? What do they see, hear, taste, and touch throughout the course of the day? Are they on your mailing list now or not? These questions can help you figure out the right communications channel for your audience and your message.

Also think about what Katya Andresen, author of *Robin Hood Marketing: Stealing Corporate Savvy to Sell Just Causes*, calls the open-minded moment. These are the times when your audience is most likely to want the benefits you are offering and to seek whatever it is you are providing. Katya says to think about open-minded moments in certain places (for example, at a grocery store or on the bus), at certain times (for example, during a heat wave or the morning commute) or in certain emotional states (for example, going through a divorce or thank-God-it's-Friday). Deliver the right message, at the right time and place, to the right person.

EXAMPLE: SELECTING CHANNELS TO REACH VOLUNTEERS

Let's take a look at which channels could work to get our four potential volunteers through the doors of our community center. Some channels will work for all of them and others will need to be tailored to the individual personas of Anna, Jessica, John, and Miguel.

First, we need to make sure that our website homepage clearly and boldly says that we are looking for new volunteers. We discussed the kinds of messages we would use to describe the volunteer opportunities in Chapter Five, so we need to make sure that our website text and images reflect those specific messages. If we have a blog, we can ask some of our existing volunteers who are similar to our personas to blog about their volunteer experiences. We will also use our email newsletter to spread the word to our existing supporters about the kind of volunteer opportunities available, again describing them in ways that will appeal to the four personas. The website, blog, and email newsletter will all be very clear that new volunteers should contact our volunteer coordinator, and we will provide her name, email address, and phone number everywhere we talk about volunteering.

Next, we'll want to drive traffic to our website by building up word-of-mouth marketing about volunteering with us. We'll think about where our personas are already going and try to get our messages out through those locations. We know that seniors like Anna hang out at the local coffee shop and the senior yoga class at the gym, so we'll go talk to the people who work there and put up some flyers. Seniors also watch TV, so we'll work on getting some publicity with our local television station.

Jessica is the single mom who is trying to build her career skills. With this persona in mind, we'll talk to counselors at the local community college and job placement centers, making sure they understand how volunteering with us can build a résumé. We'll also leave some business cards or brochures with them. We might do the same with women's groups at local churches and business associations.

Our businessman John reads the paper and has lunch with the movers and shakers in town, so we'll use personal contacts we have on staff with the Chamber of Commerce, the newspaper editor, and other business leaders in our community, encouraging them to spread the word to their friends about ways they can give back.

To reach our college student Miguel, we'll ask our existing college-age volunteers to set up social networking pages and events to spread the word to their friends. We'll also talk to counselors and popular teachers at the local community college. Perhaps we can convince some instructors to offer course credit for volunteering.

IS PRINT PASSÉ?

The same people who believe that print marketing materials are passé are probably the ones who predicted the paperless office back in the early 1990s. Personal computing has dramatically *increased* paper use, not decreased it, as everyone can now write, design, and print whatever they want, at home and at work.

How we are communicating is changing, no question about it, and that means that the role of print is changing too. The print newsletter was once the mainstay of nonprofit communications, but the email newsletter is quickly taking its place. Although a print newsletter may or may not be a good approach, print is still an important channel for many organizations. Just like any other communications channel, it depends on who you are trying to reach and what messages you are sending.

If you are trying to reach people without computers or broadband access, or people who have email but rarely check it, then an email newsletter isn't really going to work well. Many fundraising studies support using multiple channels both offline and online to raise money, particularly from older generations (such as a direct mail appeal letter and email updates with success stories).

Don't do print just because you've always done it that way. But don't write off print as an outdated channel either.

CONVINCE YOUR SUPPORTERS TO OPEN YOUR EMAIL

Email newsletters, updates, action alerts, and fundraising appeals are increasingly popular communications channels for nonprofits. But before your email newsletter will be read, it has to be opened. Here are ten tips for getting your email newsletter opened and read.

1. *Make the "From" field recognizable.* Provide consistency from issue to issue by using the same name/organization in the "From" field for each edition. Use a staff member's name if the majority of the people on the list will recognize it. Otherwise, use the organizational name or a combination of the two.

2. *Describe the candy, not the wrapper.* Use the subject line to tell us what goodies are inside this email, not about the packaging. In other words, don't put "Go Green Association Newsletter, Volume 5, Issue 7" in your subject line. Instead, tell us what's in this edition of the newsletter, such as "How to Live in Harmony with Backyard Wildlife."

3. *Change your subject line from edition to edition.* Some people will tell you that using the same subject line over and over works for them, but I believe that's probably the exception to the rule, as long as you are using a recognizable "From" field.

4. *Emphasize the personal value of your content.* It's the old "What's in it for me?" question. Why should I take precious time out of my busy day to read your email? I will, if you are providing information I want, need, or am curious about, or if reading your email will help me do something faster, cheaper, or easier or otherwise make my life more pleasant, enjoyable, or meaningful.

Subject lines that make readers think "This is useful" or "This is timely" or "This is about me" will always work.

5. *Don't tell people what to do.* Although I always recommend that you include a call to action in every email (and with every email article), some research shows that telling people what to do in the subject line itself can hurt your open rates. This is particularly true when asking people to help or donate or register. Specific calls to action are great within the body of the email, but for the subject line, lean toward the "personal value" words. For example, "Where to Dance All Night with Your Best Friends" will work better than "Register for Our All-Night Dance-a-thon Fundraiser."

6. *Keep it short.* You'll find all kinds of advice on just how many characters are optimal for email subject lines. Some go as high as sixty characters, including spaces. Somewhere around thirty-five characters seems to be the ideal now, but some people argue that even shorter is better (more like twenty characters). You can play with subject line length and see what works for you, but do try to keep it to sixty characters.

7. *Piggyback on hot topics and brand names.* Think about what's hot in the news right now. What products and services are people talking about now? How can you relate your work back to big brand names?

8. *Keep your mailing list clean.* Are you removing bouncing email addresses from your list or making sure that your email newsletter service provider does this for you? Continuously emailing bad addresses is one of the marks of a spammer, which can affect how many of your emails get delivered. Don't give the Internet service providers who trap spam for their customers a reason to block your email.

9. *Send to your list regularly.* Your supporters will recognize email from you if you send it often. Try to send email about once a month as a default schedule and adjust from there.

10. *Send in MIME.* MIME is an email format that combines an HTML version and a plain text version of your email into one message. If someone opens your email in a program that doesn't read HTML (such as many phones) or works in an office where HTML emails are blocked, they will still see your plain text version, rather than messy HTML code. Your email newsletter service provider will combine the HTML and plain text version you create into one message for you.

CONNECT WITH SUPPORTERS THROUGH MOBILE DEVICES

CTIA-The Wireless Association reported in December 2008 that 87 percent of the U.S. population had a cell phone. Also in December 2008, the Centers for Disease Control and Prevention found through its National Health Interview Survey that more than one of every five American homes (20.2 percent) had only wireless telephones—no landlines at all. Worldwide, the International Telecommunications Union reports there are a mere 1.27 billion fixed lines, compared to 2.68 billion mobile accounts. All of this means that you should consider asking your clients and supporters for their cell phone numbers and obtaining permission to send them text messages.

"Mobile access strengthens the three pillars of online engagement: Connecting with others, satisfying information queries, and sharing content with others," says John B. Horrigan, associate director of the Pew Internet and American Life Project. In an April 2009 report, Pew found that African-Americans are the fastest-growing group among those adopting the mobile technology. The percentage of African-Americans using mobile phones or another type of connected gadget to share email, exchange instant messages, and access the Internet for information on an average day had more than doubled since late 2007, helping to close the digital divide. That means that in addition to reaching people on their cell phones, you should also consider creating a mobile-friendly version of your website.

Barack Obama's presidential campaign amassed a list of about one million cell numbers and used text messages for special campaign announcements like the selection of Joe Biden as the vice presidential candidate and to push voter turnout. Campaign staff relied on cell phones to reach people who are less likely to be on a computer regularly, including young people, minorities, and the poor, says Colin Delany of epolitics.com. If these trends hold true, you may very well be using mobile technology to communicate with a large percentage of your clients, supporters, and other interested people in the coming years. Prepare now by starting to collect cell phone numbers.

CONCLUSION: FIND THE RIGHT MIX AND GIVE IT TIME TO WORK

The most creative, focused message won't motivate a single person if it's not delivered to your target audience in a format they are likely to see. We are all inundated with information and messaging in all aspects of our lives. Even if the right message appears in the right place, if it only appears there once it can be easily overlooked. Find the right mix of words, images, and communications tools to share your message with your target audience, then stick with your marketing plan. Give it ample time to work. You'll tire of your nonprofit marketing program before your audience will!

chapter **SEVEN**

Spread Your Message Further by Telling Great Stories

Tell me a story, kid.

—Don Hewitt, creator of *60 Minutes*

This chapter is about . . .

- The power of storytelling in nonprofit marketing
- Three specific inspirational plots that nonprofits can use
- Where to find good stories and how to use them

One of the most effective yet underused nonprofit marketing techniques is storytelling. We touched briefly on storytelling in Chapter Six as we looked at packaging your message into words, but we didn't look at exactly how you tell a great story, so let's do that now.

Telling stories about your cause to your supporters works so well because, as Chip Heath and Dan Heath—authors of *Made to Stick* (a book I highly recommend to nonprofit communicators)—would say, stories are sticky. They are easier to remember than statistics, making it more likely that our friends will share the story with their friends, creating free word-of-mouth marketing. Stories also help us put a human face on the numbers behind the need, which is essential in fundraising. As the Heath brothers say, stories work because they provide both *simulation*, which is the knowledge about how to act, and *inspiration*, which is the motivation to act.

ADD "STORYTELLER" TO YOUR JOB DESCRIPTION

I suspect that one of the reasons nonprofits are not using storytelling as much as they could is because nonprofit staff simply don't see themselves as professional storytellers. A storyteller, they think, is an incredible writer like Shakespeare. Or some jolly older gentleman with a long white beard and colorful pants at the children's library. Or someone with a master of fine arts degree who goes away on long writing retreats.

The good news is that you don't have to be any of those people to use storytelling effectively. Good nonprofit marketing stories come in all shapes and sizes. Take the Doritos bag I spotted on my kitchen counter one day. On the back of the bag was this story:

> Divine [Bradley] noticed a lack of resources for the kids growing up in his rough Brooklyn neighborhood, so he brought the problem home with him, literally. At 17, he converted his basement into a community center to give teens in his neighborhood something they sorely needed: options. Divine's organization, Team Revolution, now provides career and financial literacy training. His workshops empower kids to take charge of their lives. The revolution has begun.

It's a great little nonprofit story on the back of a Doritos bag. If nonprofit storytelling works there, you can use your stories anywhere.

You have plenty of material—all nonprofits do. Nonprofits are sitting on a goldmine of stories, because you are trying to bring about important changes in people's lives and in the way the world looks, thinks, and works. Anytime you seek change, you invite conflict, and conflict always makes for a great story! Your challenge is to know how to spot those rough nuggets of gold and to polish them up into stories that you can use in your communications and marketing to connect more effectively with potential and current supporters.

Made to Stick identifies three story plots considered to be the most inspirational: the *challenge plot*, the *creativity plot*, and the *connection plot*. I've reviewed hundreds of nonprofit stories and broken down the elements of these three plotlines in detail, so you can understand how to use them, even if you don't believe storytelling comes to you naturally. Keep in mind that mixing and matching elements from the three plots is perfectly fine. For example, you'll often see elements of a challenge plot in a creativity plot story and vice versa.

ON THE WEB To see several real examples of how nonprofits are using these three plot lines and using stories in their marketing campaigns, visit the companion website.

TELL STORIES WITH THE CHALLENGE PLOT

The challenge plot is the most recognizable plot line, and that's because virtually every Hollywood movie uses it. To mix a few metaphors, these are the classic American stories of the underdog who, against all odds, goes from rags to riches. These stories inspire us to act and to get involved. They appeal to our courage and our strength, and they give us confidence that what we're trying to do really will work. These stories are very empowering for your donors and your volunteers.

The challenge plot follows the classic three-act structure. In Act I, we learn about our protagonist, who should be an individual rather than a group of people. We get some details about his situation and his goals. We want to know this is a real person you're talking about, so provide some details about the setting, such as where he is living, what month and year it is, and so on. We have to understand where this person is headed, or wants to be headed, and get a sense for the barriers that stand in the way.

Here's a simple example that could come from thousands of social service agencies: *A sixteen-year-old boy named Jamal leaves home in Los Angeles because his drug-addicted mother beats him and hasn't been to a grocery store in months. But living on the streets is tough, and Jamal resorts to mugging people to stay alive.* We can visualize our protagonist in our mind's eye. We understand that he wants a better life than the one his mother is providing, but he's having a hard time on his own.

In Act II, obstacles and conflict appear. The protagonist may overcome some of the smaller obstacles in his way, but we eventually see him falling to a low, and we aren't sure how the story will turn out. The tension mounts. It looks as though a villainous someone or something may prevent our hero from reaching his goals.

Back to our story: *Jamal is arrested and released several times, and after a few months on his own, he decides that life in jail is easier than life on the streets. In jail, you still have to fight to protect yourself, but at least you get three hots and a cot. He thinks sometimes about stabbing someone to get a longer sentence, but he really doesn't want to hurt anyone.* We see our character reaching a terrible low: this young man now believes that a long jail sentence is his best option. The unspoken villain is a society that lets young people like Jamal fall through the cracks and picks them up only long enough to put them in the penal system.

Finally, in Act III, the action peaks. The final obstacle is overcome and we get the big payoff: the protagonist reaches his goals. We see how this person persevered and triumphed. Close strongly, with a great result. We want to really see the protagonist achieve his goals, with a hopeful outlook for the future.

Here's how our story ends: *Marcus, a Hope House counselor who ten years earlier had been in much the same situation as Jamal, sees Jamal trying to shoplift food one day. He offers to buy the kid lunch, then explains that Hope House is a transitional living center that can help Jamal get off the street, allowing him to get his GED and find a job so that he can support himself, legally. "The people at Hope House believed in me and gave me a second chance at a real life. That's all I really needed," says Jamal.*

Did you notice where the nonprofit in our story came in? In Act III, as a supporting character. The story is still about the protagonist, and it ends with his success. The best challenge plot stories are not about your nonprofit but about someone you are serving. Go back to your mission statement: why do you exist and who do you serve? Those people and their problems are the basis of Acts I and II. Although human service agencies will have the easiest time with this plot, all nonprofits can use it. Make the story about the people who will be impacted by your work or your partnerships, even if you don't work directly with those people.

TELL STORIES WITH THE CREATIVITY PLOT

Creativity plots are about those big "Aha!" moments in which we reach a breakthrough that solves a nagging problem. They can also be "What if?" stories that encourage people to think about old problems in entirely new and creative ways. If your organization is advocating a different kind of approach to a well-understood problem or talks a lot about "thinking outside the box," the creativity plot will work well for you.

Creativity plots start with a well-understood problem and a typical, commonplace response to that problem that just doesn't work. Let's look at an excerpt from the story behind the founding of Heifer International, as told on their website, as an example of a classic creativity plot.

> A farmer named Dan West was ladling out rations of milk to hungry children during the Spanish Civil War when it hit him. "These children don't need a cup. They need a cow." West, who was serving as a Church of the Brethren relief worker, was forced to decide who would receive the limited rations and who wouldn't. This kind of aid, he knew, would never be enough.

The well-understood problem is clear: starving children. The old approach that just isn't working is clear too: rations dispensed in food lines.

The second half of the creativity plot is the new, innovative approach to the old problem—and the promise it holds for creating a new reality. In many of these stories, the new approach has yet to be fully proven. Test runs and theories are fine, but it's important to close with the big vision of the problem solved, just like in the challenge plot where you need to close with the individual's triumph.

The Heifer International story continues:

> West returned home to form Heifers for Relief, dedicated to ending hunger permanently by providing families with livestock and training so they could be spared the indignity of depending on others to feed their children. . . . This simple idea of giving families a source of food, rather than short-term relief, caught on and has continued for over 60 years. Since 1944, Heifer has helped 8.5 million people in more than 125 countries.

Here we see the creative solution: Don't given them a cup of milk, give them the cow that's going to produce over and over. Give heifers, female livestock, that will produce offspring that can be shared with others in the community. It's an entirely new way of fighting an old problem, and it's now spread worldwide. It's a classic creativity plot.

TELL STORIES WITH THE CONNECTION PLOT

Connection plots are what you might call bridging-the-gap stories, because they are often about unlikely connections. These stories are often about a small, seemingly inconsequential event with a surprise twist that ends up revealing some kind of universal truth or lesson. They can also make you think, "There but for the grace of God go I." Stories with a connection plot may be the hardest of the three to write, but they are also the most emotionally powerful. These stories, when done well, can work wonders in fundraising letters.

Take a look at this blog post from Interplast, a nonprofit that performs surgeries on cleft palate defects and burn injuries in developing countries. It's written in the voice of Janet Volpe, one of the doctors on the trip.

> This is Van Canh with his wife and 9-month-old daughter, Thi Sang Sang. Thi Sang Sang was born with a cleft lip, like her father. When Van Canh heard that Interplast was coming to Cao Lanh, he and his wife decided, despite financial hardship, to leave their family store for the day and make the two-hour bus journey to our clinic day to have their daughter evaluated. Fourteen years ago, Interplast operated on clefts on both sides of Van Canh's mouth. He had been told he would need a revision in the future, but because of work and family commitments, he had never been able to make it back for the revision. As our team evaluated Thi Sang Sang, we asked Van Canh if he'd like to have his clefts revised during our stay. He and his wife were overjoyed that we would consider this for him. At the age of 26 years, he told us he thought he was too old for Interplast to want to perform another surgery on him, and had no money to have the revision performed locally. We scheduled the surgeries one day apart, and this photo was taken at the time of discharge from the hospital. Van Canh had brought chewing gum from his store; just before going home, he gave each member of our team a stick as a token of appreciation. I taped my Wrigley's Doublemint wrapper in my journal and will always remember this kind and grateful family.

Connection plots often start with a small specific situation or event that may not be particularly noteworthy on its own. But as the story progresses, a connection to a greater, universal human experience is revealed. This often comes through a surprise, a discovery, or some kind of epiphany. We see connections between the characters in these stories, but also between the person listening to the story and the people in it.

In the Interplast story, the small, specific situation was the father bringing his daughter in for the surgery. Interplast could have written this up focusing on the little girl, and it could have been a nice success story that demonstrates the work they do. But then we get the twist: the father went through this same experience as a child, but still needed another surgery. Now Interplast is offering to perform his surgery too.

The human connection is about gratitude. The father giving all he could—a stick of gum—was all the Interplast team needed to feel the family's appreciation. The doctor was so touched that she kept her gum wrapper, reminding her to be grateful for everything she has, and reminding us of the same thing as we read the story.

USE THE SIX QUALITIES OF A GOOD NONPROFIT MARKETING STORY

You need more than a good plot for a story to work in nonprofit marketing. Strive for these six qualities in your stories.

Short. Take only as long to tell the story as you really need to. If you are telling a story online, try for five hundred words. If you are producing a video, no more than two minutes is ideal.

Straightforward. Be clear and straightforward. Don't try to do too much. Avoid going off on tangents, even if they seem interesting, because they will detract from the main reason you are telling the story.

Personal. Your stories should be about specific people, not general stand-ins for a larger population. Make it personal. Limit the number of people in the story. In the Interplast example, we don't learn much about the doctor, other than her narrative voice and her reaction to the stick of gum. Nor do we hear much at all about the wife or the daughter. The story is primarily about the father, and it focuses our attention on the connections with him.

Authentic. We connect with stories that ring true. We don't want to hear stories about impossibly perfect people. We hate those people! We want to hear about the people who are like us, human and imperfect, making mistakes and learning from those mistakes. We want to hear about real people, even if their names or other identifying characteristics are changed to protect their privacy.

Includes conflict or imperfections. Conflict and imperfections are what bring stories to life and make us care about how they turn out. That sometimes means providing unflattering details about clients. If you work in social services, your stories will often include drug abuse and criminal activities. But we have to understand the complicated and rough histories in order to see how amazing the transformation of the person in the story truly is.

Ends with a message. Although storytelling is a wonderful tool for nonprofit marketing, it works only when you have a specific goal in mind. Make sure that the message of your story is clear. You don't necessarily need to say, "And this story means that . . ." The story itself should make that clear. Your readers or listeners should understand what they are supposed to be feeling and what they are supposed to do next.

FIND FRESH STORY IDEAS

When the blank computer screen is staring back at you, knowing *what* to write about (or talk about on a podcast or video) can be challenging, even if you understand *how* to write a story using one of the three plots we reviewed. Here are my ten favorite sources of story ideas for nonprofit communicators. Keep in mind that these are places to look for inspiration and story ideas, not necessarily for the story content itself. Don't violate anyone's copyrights by using their content without permission.

1. *The receptionist's desk.* Ask whoever answers your organization's main phone number for the top three questions callers ask, then turn the answers into stories for your newsletter, blog, and other messaging.
2. *Your clients' and supporters' lives.* Ask the people your organization helps about what's happening in their lives right now, what questions they are pondering or what decisions they are making. Ask some of your supporters the same thing. Ask them to explain what their situation was like before working with your organization and what it's like now. You can also survey your donors, clients, or members about the issues they care about.
3. *Your newsletter or blog archives.* What did you write about this time last year? Can you freshen up an old article or provide a timely update on something you've covered before?
4. *The headlines.* Look at the last week's worth of headlines from your local newspaper or the website of your favorite national TV news network or

news magazine. What issues are they covering and how are those news items related to your work?

5. *Your desk calendar.* Think about hooks tied into holidays and other special days on the calendar. There are hundreds of specially designated weeks and months. For example, June is Adopt a Shelter Cat Month, National Iced Tea Month, and Rebuild Your Life Month. Chase's Calendar of Events is the ultimate source for all such occasions, but you can find many lists free online.
6. *Your web stats.* Look at your website statistics and you'll find what keywords people are typing into search engines before they direct traffic to your website. Take those phrases and write detailed articles on those topics.
7. *Trade news aggregators.* Services like Alltop.com collect blog posts and group them into specific categories, including Animal Rescue, Child Healthcare, Education, Museums, and most likely some topic related to your good cause too. Subject-oriented news aggregators are a great way to not only see trends in what others are writing about but also find out what's hot right now.
8. *Event programs.* See who's talking about what at various conferences, workshops, and webinars related to your work. Ask to interview those experts or ask whether they'd like to submit a guest post.
9. *Twitter and SlideShare.* These two social media sites are particularly well known as places where people share interesting content with other users—links to interesting articles and blog posts on Twitter and Microsoft PowerPoint slide decks on SlideShare. Search on your keywords and see what people are thinking about and suggesting to others.
10. *Social bookmarking sites.* Users of websites like Delicious, Digg, and Stumble Upon tag the content they like as they find it on the web. Search on your keywords to find articles related to your work.

INTERVIEW YOUR SUPPORTERS FOR PROFILES AND STORIES

Nonprofit stories often take the form of personal profiles of people associated with the organization. You'll often find them under headings like Volunteer Spotlight, Friends of (Your Issue), and Meet the Board. Nonprofits also use profiles to put a specific human face on their programs, accomplishments, needs, and advocacy positions.

Every good profile starts with an interview. Here are ten tips I've learned after writing many a profile over the years:

1. *Don't ask for information you can easily get elsewhere.* Do your homework. Don't ask your board chair where she works or what her title is. Don't ask a donor how much he has given your organization. You should already have that information. It's OK to ask people to *confirm* the spelling of their names or if the total amount donated over several years sounds right to them, but this should be presented as quick fact-checking, not as part of the interview.

2. *Don't fall into Tedious Bio Syndrome.* It's the narrative equivalent of a résumé. Or worse, you start when they were born. Profiles that start that way are total snoozers, and so are the interviews themselves.

3. *Be flexible about the format.* You can get the information you need whether you conduct the interview in person, over the phone, or via email. I find it's actually easier to take good notes while interviewing over the phone, rather than in person, because I don't have to worry about maintaining eye contact, and I can type much faster than I can write. Invest in a good, comfortable headset for hands-free phone conversations. People who are a bit nervous about being interviewed often prefer email, because it gives them time to mull over their answers.

4. *Prepare a list of questions, but be willing to stray from it.* Come up with some good questions to get the conversation going, but don't be afraid to ask new questions or take the interview in a different direction, as long as you are getting good details and quotes. Listen for intriguing details or good sound bites and follow them.

5. *Ask open-ended questions that contain emotional words.* Fact-filled profiles simply aren't as interesting as those full of feeling and emotion. To get your subject to provide you with good anecdotes and quotes, ask questions that are variations on "How did that make you feel?" Try questions like "What has surprised you most about . . . ?" "What upsets you most about . . . ?" and "What do you remember most about . . . ?"

6. *Don't be a gushing fan.* It's fine if you admire the person you are talking to, but don't interview them as a fan. You'll end up writing the worst kind of profile: the Obvious Kiss-Up. Be nice to your VIPs, but don't overdo it.

7. *If you are writing the story with a specific purpose in mind, ask some leading questions.* For example, if you are profiling Mrs. Smith because she put your nonprofit in her will, and you want to encourage others to do the same, you need to ask Mrs. Smith some leading questions to elicit the right kind of quotes. For example, you might ask, "Why did you select our nonprofit specifically when you could have left your gift to any group?" and "How did you feel after you made the decision?" Asking donors about the kind of legacy they want to leave behind can also work well.

8. *Don't go astray with entertaining but irrelevant stories.* Sometimes you'll interview someone who loves to talk and tell you funny stories about all of their friends. Although it might be a very entertaining conversation for both of you, you will end up with little that you can use in your profile. Warming up to each other with stories about crazy adventures abroad are fine, but then steer the conversation back to the subject of the profile.

9. *Give the interviewee control over the content.* This is not hard news or "gotcha" journalism. You are profiling people because you care about them and because they care about your cause. Ask whether your profile subject would like to see the story you write before it is published (most will say yes). Give them a few days to get back to you with any changes they feel are important. This ensures not only that you have your facts straight, but also that your supporters are pleased with the way they are portrayed in your communications.

10. *Follow up within a few days with any additional questions.* Don't wait too long after your original interview to write the profile. That way you can quickly follow up with additional questions while the conversation is still fresh in both of your minds.

PROTECT THE PRIVACY OF THE PEOPLE IN YOUR STORIES

Many nonprofits must wrangle with legal and ethical issues when talking about the people they serve. But don't use confidentiality requirements as an excuse for avoiding storytelling. You can approach this challenge in several different ways.

Get permission. Simply ask the person if it's OK to tell his or her story, or if you need something more formal (good for potentially controversial or otherwise touchy topics), ask the person to sign a release. You can find sample release language by searching online for "story release form" or "model release form." Write the story, complete with the level of detail you would like to share. Let the subject of the story read it and make any desired edits. When you explain how you'll be using the story to build support for your agency, many people are not only flattered but also pleased to be able to give back in this way.

Change identifying details. You can change elements of the story that are not central to it in order to protect someone's identity. You can change the person's name, location, age, and other demographics that are irrelevant to the outcome of the story.

Create a composite. You can combine elements of more than one person's story into a new fictional character. However, be careful not to present this person as a real human being. Instead, open your story with language like, "Imagine if you were a . . ." or "What if . . ." By using this approach, you are making the story more about the listeners or readers and asking your audience to put themselves in the shoes of someone else. Ensure that your composite still rings true and sounds as if it could be a real person in your community, even if it isn't.

INCORPORATE STORIES INTO YOUR COMMUNICATIONS

Here are ten specific ways you can use stories in your day-to-day communications:

1. *Include a story about a real person in every speech you give.* Talking to potential volunteers? Tell a story or two about real volunteers and the difference they are making in the lives of others.

2. *Turn a story into a how-to article for your newsletter.* Using the first person ("How I . . ."), have someone on your staff, a board member, or a volunteer explain how to do something, based on that person's own experience in learning how to do it.

3. *Include testimonials in your event marketing.* Ask people who attended your workshop to provide testimonials about how they personally used what they learned at the event in their own work.

4. *Single out one person you are helping in your next fundraising appeal letter.* Instead of talking broadly about the need for low-cost childcare in your community, talk about the plight of just one single mom.

5. *Use serial storytelling on a campaign blog.* Hook in readers with frequent updates about a particular person, animal, or item. Environmental and humane

groups use this tactic effectively all the time (such as tracking a particular whale's journey—"Will he evade the evil whale hunters?"—or profiling a dog that has been badly abused, but is now on the mend after being rescued—"Will she live? And walk again?").

6. *Give each board member at least one good story to use.* Your board members should be advocating for your organization at all times. Give them real stories they can use that will put your organization in a good light with potential donors, volunteers, community decision makers, and so on. Make time on your next board meeting agenda to hear stories and to practice telling them.

7. *Lead your next press release with a story.* The media loves real stories, so use them as angles in your press releases. If you can make the real person in the story available for interviews, that's even better.

8. *Incorporate a story into a training session.* Who do you train? Volunteers, new staff, community members, others in your field? Incorporate a good story into your next training session.

9. *Add stories to your annual report.* They can take the form of personal profiles, first-person accounts, or short testimonials, but include stories about real people in your annual report to reinforce the narrative about your accomplishments and activities.

10. *Rotate stories on your website home page.* Collect stories about specific people related to your organization and rotate them on your home page.

CONCLUSION: STORIES ARE A NONPROFIT'S GOLDMINE

If you are not using storytelling as an essential element in your nonprofit marketing and communications, you are robbing yourself of one of the most effective tools available to you.

"No matter whether I'm working on a newsletter or being interviewed by a reporter, I always think 'Tell a story,'" says Lane Phalen of the TAILS Humane Society in DeKalb, Illinois. "Why do we need donations to build an outdoor fence for dogs? Chip, a retriever mix, needs to stretch his legs to relieve energy so he can remain in his kennel for the other twenty-three hours of the day. Why do we need extra donations to pay medical bills? Missy, a black cat left at our doorstep, had a gnarled and broken leg that was so bad, we had to amputate it. But then we got her back in good health and found a home for her."

Telling stories makes the needs and the successes of your organization real to your supporters.

Nonprofits are story goldmines. You now know the elements of three inspirational plot lines that work well for nonprofits, where to look for stories, and where to use them. Take the time to do some mining. Stop and look for those rough rocks and polish them up into beautiful gems. Wear them yourself and share them with others every day.

PART THREE

Building a Community of Supporters Around You

No matter what your mission statement says, all nonprofits share a common goal: to get certain people to think, feel, or act differently because you believe it will lead to some public good. You may want people to change their behavior or attitudes. You may want lawmakers or regulators to change policies. You may want your supporters to take certain actions or to donate their time or money. You may want to research, educate, or raise awareness about particular issues. These are big goals that will be hard to accomplish on your own.

But when you make nonprofit marketing a core part of your organizational management, you don't have to do it alone. Instead, you build a community of supporters (what many in small business marketing are now calling a *tribe*) around you. Nonprofit communications directors are turning into nonprofit community builders, organizers, and managers, as nonprofits recognize the value in letting their supporters connect with each other and the nonprofit's staff and volunteer leaders more regularly and more personally. As you build this community around you, you exponentially grow the number of people who are now helping you market your good cause.

In this section, you'll look at some of the basic steps in building your network of supporters: making it easy for people to find and to connect with your cause (Chapter Eight), becoming an expert that the media and others turn to (Chapter Nine), staying in touch with your supporters through frequent communications (Chapter Ten), adopting an attitude of gratitude toward your supporters (Chapter Eleven), and empowering your fans to build even more support for you (Chapter Twelve). Sounds good, doesn't it?

chapter
EIGHT

Make It Easy to Find You and to Connect with Your Cause

If you wish to win a man over to your ideas,
first make him your friend.

—Abraham Lincoln

This chapter is about . . .

- Being visible so people can find your organization
- Creating your online presence
- Offering new contacts multiple ways to stay in touch

Few people wake up and decide out of the blue to support a particular charity. It's much more likely that one of two scenarios will happen: the person will be referred to you by a trusted source, or the person will seek out an organization that can help her in some way.

In the first scenario, the person might hear about you from a friend who was talking over lunch about volunteering with your organization (we call that word-of-mouth marketing). Or your organization might be included in a story on the evening news program that this person watches every day (we call that publicity).

Either way, this potential new supporter learns about your organization from a trusted source; what she hears piques her interest, and she seeks out additional informational about you.

In the second scenario, an event in a person's life, big or small, prompts her to seek answers to questions she has or motivates her to take some kind of action in her own life. Few people would think, "I want to find an animal rescue group and give them some money." Instead, they are much more likely to think, "I'm really tired of all the stray cats coming into our yard. We need to do something about this. I wonder who can help me?" Or "I'm ready to give in and get the kids a puppy. Where should I get one and what kind?" She connects with your mission or your programs and services before she connects with your organization itself, because it's your mission that meets some kind of need or touches on some values in her own life.

In both scenarios, you want this person to be able to easily find your organization, regardless of whether she heard about you from a trusted source or is trying to resolve a question or problem in her own life. Once she finds you, you want to offer ways to stay in touch with each other and to open the lines for two-way communication.

CREATE A VISIBLE AND ACCESSIBLE HOME BASE

Every nonprofit should have a primary home base. This is the place where you want people to start when contacting you for the first time. You'll put this on every publication you create. It's also the contact information that you want your current supporters to pass on to their friends. When they are having dinner together, and one friend mentions your organization to another, what do you want that person to write down on the cocktail napkin about how to contact you?

Your home base may be a physical location that you own or rent, where clients and supporters come regularly. In that case, you'll constantly promote your street address or easily identifiable location (for example, 1255 Main Street in Smithtown, or across the street from Smithtown Elementary School).

But many nonprofits don't have public offices or rarely have in-person visitors. Others use P.O. boxes, which people obviously can't visit. In these cases, promoting a physical address doesn't make much sense, because it doesn't allow that potential new supporter or client to find you quickly. Instead, you should emphasize a phone number, email address, or website as your primary home base. For example, if you run a hotline, your toll-free phone number is a more appropriate home base to promote. If your staff are spread out across the country or work from home offices, using your website as your home base will make more sense.

Your home base should be the primary point of contact for newcomers. Whichever home base you choose, whether it's a street address, phone number, or a website domain, plaster it everywhere that a person interested in your work would reasonably look for you. When you have space, it's fine to include your complete contact information. But you'll often be required to include much less, and in these cases, go with that visible and accessible home base.

BE WHERE PEOPLE ARE SEARCHING FOR ORGANIZATIONS LIKE YOURS

Once you have decided on your primary home base, you need to make sure that it is highly visible. Be where people would expect to find you. Ensure that you are listed in phone books and other local directories like Chamber of Commerce listings, both offline and online. Local governments that rely on nonprofits to perform vital community services will often include links to you on their websites, as well as on their 2-1-1 referral lists. Also think about which community groups or associations someone might contact in search of an organization like yours. Are you in their membership directories or on their referral lists?

You also need to be on the tip of the tongue of experts in your communities, whether geographic, professional, or topical. Recommendations from personal acquaintances are the most trusted form of advertising, according to a July 2009 Nielsen Global Online Consumer Survey of over twenty-five thousand Internet consumers from fifty countries. Ninety percent of consumers surveyed said they trust recommendations from people they know, and 70 percent trusted consumer opinions posted online, even if they didn't know the person.

What our friends, even mere acquaintances, tell us matters—a lot.

Do your best to make sure that when people ask their friends for a recommendation related to your mission, those friends mention your name and home base. Some people are more likely than others to be asked for recommendations on a particular issue. If you want to know about environmentally friendly household cleaners, you are more likely to ask someone who drives a Prius or tends an organic vegetable garden than someone who drives a gas guzzler or sprays chemicals on their lawn.

Building up your word-of-mouth referrals takes time, but it can be a very powerful form of marketing for nonprofits. In fact, it's probably the best form of marketing because it's free (or relatively cheap) and it's trusted.

The Word of Mouth Marketing Association defines the basics of word-of-mouth marketing as

- Educating people about your products and services
- Identifying people most likely to share their opinion
- Providing tools that make it easier to share information
- Studying how, where, and when opinions are being shared
- Listening and responding to supporters, detractors, and neutrals[1]

Using this list as a guide, think about ways you can encourage your current supporters to tell others about your organization.

Let's say we work on animal issues in our community. If we run a public animal shelter, then we'll use the shelter address as our primary home base. In all of our marketing campaigns, we'll always make sure our street address is clear.

But what if we don't have a facility and instead are a network of people who provide foster care for animals until we can find homes for them? Even though we have a P.O. box, we aren't going to emphasize that. Instead, we'll connect with people primarily through our website, so that's what we'll promote as our primary home base.

Which directories should we be listed in? What would people do if they either found or lost a pet? Who would they call for recommendations? Here are some of the likely people and places our nonprofit should be in touch with, so they know who we are and the best way for people to reach us.

Government agencies. Most local governments have a department that handles animal control issues. They may respond only in emergency situations, but we'd want whoever answers that phone number to know we exist and to offer us as a resource for people calling about lost or found pets.

Professionals who work with animals. We should contact every veterinary office, pet shop, dog walker, pet sitter, and groomer in our area and keep them updated on how we can help their customers.

Other animal charities. We should contact every other animal-related group we know, even if they don't deal with cats and dogs, including equestrian groups.

Remember, if I've lost a dog, and I have the choice to ask a friend for suggestions, I'll pick the friend who has horses over one who has no pets at all.

UNFAMILIAR WITH SOME OF THE TERMS IN THIS CHAPTER?

If you find some of the terminology in this section foreign or confusing, refer to the Glossary of Online Marketing Terms at the back of the book.

GET YOUR WEBSITE IN GOOD SHAPE

The first friend that many of us turn to when we have questions these days isn't our college roommate, but Google or another search engine. You want to make sure that Google and other search engines produce *your* site as a top answer to the searcher's question. You do that in part by having a decent website that you update regularly and that others link to.

The days when your nonprofit could get away with not having an online presence are gone. Even the smallest or most locally based organizations are expected to use email and have a website. If you don't, your audience will immediately assume—rightly or wrongly—that your organization is run by amateurs or fly-by-nights.

Your website is the trunk of your online marketing tree. Everything you do online grows from and connects back to your website. Potential new supporters will also form their first impressions of you through your website, so make it a good one (the website and the first impression). I recommend the following ten-point checklist of questions to ask as you evaluate your current website or guide the creation of a new one.

1. Does the Domain Name Make Sense?

Use whole words if they are relatively short. Abbreviations can work too. For example, the Environmental Defense Fund can be found at edf.org. Environmentaldefense.org and environmentaldefensefund.org redirect automatically to edf.org. Note that their domain name is not some difficult-to-recall abbreviation like envdef.org. Those are the worst, because they are very difficult to guess and to remember. Shorter is better, because you'll leave less room for typos.

You should also consider purchasing multiple domain names as EDF has done. In real estate, it's location, location, location. Online, those locations are your domain names. I recommend that nonprofits buy not only the .org versions of their domain names, but also the .com and .net versions. When you don't buy all the versions, someone else will eventually snatch them up and most likely put up an advertising site. If the domains you want are not currently available, you can establish a monitoring account with your domain registrar so you'll be notified if the current owners let their domain registrations lapse, making them publicly available again.

Also consider purchasing domain names that feature your keywords, project names, and so on. You can either forward these domains to your main website or you can use them to create and market microsites, or mini-websites that may or may not be part of your larger website. For example, the Humane Society of the United States operates microsites on StopPuppyMills.org, HumaneTeen.org, and several other campaign-specific domain addresses.

2. Do I Know Where I Am?

Can I tell after the briefest glance whose website I'm on? Are your logo and name right at the top? If your organization works only locally or regionally, it's also important that we quickly see exactly where you are. Include your city and state in a prominent location. This will help site visitors who may easily mistake you for a similar organization in a different area. For example, I live in Davidson County, North Carolina, but there is also a Davidson County, Tennessee, which includes Nashville. Nonprofits in areas with common place names should be very clear and upfront on their home pages about which state they are in, especially when the place name is within the name of the organization.

3. Is There a Clear Path to Answers or Actions Visitors Are Most Likely Seeking?

To help focus your site on your visitors rather than on your organization itself, think about why people would come to your website in the first place. What three questions would they be seeking answers for? What three actions would they like to take (say, registering for an event, exploring your services, donating online)? The path to those answers and actions should be crystal clear on your home page. Within just a few seconds, can I see where I need to click to get those answers and take those actions?

Creating this kind of website requires that you understand your target audience well. Your website should reflect those people—the website visitors—more than it reflects the people who work at the nonprofit or the organization itself. You can achieve this by structuring the navigation of your website around the top answers they are seeking and actions they'd like to take.

The website of Family Service Association of Bucks County, Pennsylvania, used to be a good example of what we call "brochure-ware." The site was designed around a list of programs and services, most of which were described in social service jargon. Content on the home page focused on organizational news like receiving a grant or asking people to sign up for events. The site was more focused on the organization than on its users.

In late 2009, Family Service Association gave the site a complete makeover. Now, instead of focusing on programs, it focuses on people. Big, up-close photos of the kinds of people that Family Service Association is helping dominate the homepage, with plain-English descriptions of what the agency does. The wording in the navigational menus and text includes "we" and "you," which creates a much more personal experience for users.

"Family Service is a very complex agency and because of that, our biggest marketing challenge has always been how to explain what we do and our impact in the community in an easy, understandable way," says Stephanie Sides, communications coordinator. "We decided the best way to tell our story was through simple conversational language using client stories to show the impact. The site is now all about people—the people whose lives we improve and the people who help us achieve our mission."

4. Does the Home Page Include Images?

The web is a visual place, and every home page should include at least one image. Ideally, you will use your own photography, but if good photos aren't available, you can use high-quality stock photography too. Choose photos that make an impression on site visitors and give them additional information about your organization's work.

5. Can I Donate Online Easily from the Home Page?

Don't hide that Donate Now button where we have to search for it. Make it very easy to find, and make it easy for supporters to fill out your online form by keeping the amount of required information to a minimum.

6. Are You Capturing Email Addresses?

Getting people to your website is the hard part. Now that you've got them there, don't let them just disappear back into cyberspace. The best way to turn a first-time website visitor into a long-term supporter is to start a conversation. To do that, you have to know who they are. Encourage visitors to stay in touch with you by signing up for an email newsletter, action alerts, or whatever you'd like to call your email correspondence. Make signing up for your email newsletter incredibly easy and obvious. Or offer a free download that requires registration. The point is to capture those email addresses so you can start a conversation with those website visitors.

7. Are People Featured?

Every nonprofit, even those focused on saving whales, needs to have people pictures and stories on its website. Donors write checks to support the work of people trying to save the whales, not the whales themselves. Whale pictures are fine, but also feature your donors, volunteers, staff, partners, clients, and other people on your website doing the work they love on behalf of your cause.

8. Are There Stories on the Need or Successes?

Mission statements are usually tough to understand because they are written in jargon or nonprofit-ese that only insiders like staff and board members can understand. Yet that's often exactly what nonprofits post on their home pages, leaving your average website visitor confused about what it is you actually do.

In stark contrast, stories draw people in and really explain what it is you do. Stories are the easiest ways to give examples of the need for your organization, the challenges you face, what you are doing to overcome them, and your successes. Tell short stories on your home page or link from your home page excerpts to the full story elsewhere on your website.

TAILS Humane Society in DeKalb, Illinois, saw immediate results when it began posting stories on its website. "Our website had about eight thousand visitors each month, but when I posted the adorable faces of pets looking for homes and told a short story about each one's background and personality on the main page of our website, our visitors steadily grew to more than eighteen thousand each month," says Lane Phalen, a board member and public relations committee chair. "Now I feature a dog, cat, and little critter on the main page all the time and change the pets twice weekly. I added a column called 'Your TAILS Tales' where I post stories and photos of pets who have been adopted from TAILS, written by their new owners. I'm always running into people who tell me they read those stories all the time."

9. Is It Easy to Contact Staff?

Before a donor writes a big check, that person will probably want to talk to you. If someone is interested in partnering with your organization, that person will want to know which staff person to call to discuss a project. Don't make it hard to identify who's doing what. If you don't want to include staff email addresses on your web page because of spam concerns, at least include a contact form and the phone numbers of key staff. A full staff directory is ideal.

10. Regularly Delete Out-of-Date Content

Outdated information on your website is the equivalent of mail and newspapers stacking up at the curb. Anybody in there? Everything OK? Let the world know that you are alive and well by keeping your website current.

IMPROVE YOUR SEARCH ENGINE RANKINGS

Enter virtually any term into a search engine like Google, Yahoo! or Bing, and you'll get back thousands, if not millions, of results. But what appears on the first page of results is most important. A 2008 study by the search engine marketing firm iProspect found that 49 percent of people look at only the first page of results; if they don't find what they are looking for on the first page, they'll change their search terms or search engine. That means you need to optimize your site for the search engines for those keywords that are most important to you, so that your site appears on the first page when someone searches on those terms.

What do you think your site is about? Do Google and other search engines agree with you? After creating your list of keywords (review Chapter Three if you need some tips on creating your keyword list), compare that list to what Google thinks your site is about by using their free keyword tool (search on "Google External Keyword Tool" to find it online).

Following the advice in the preceding ten-point checklist will help you improve your search engine rankings, because people are more likely to link to high-quality sites with up-to-date, interesting content. But there are also many small changes you can make, some editorial and some technical, that can also increase your search engine rankings.

Put Keywords in the Right Places in Your Page Text

After you develop a list of keywords for your site, putting those keywords in particular places will help search engines recognize them as meaningful. Use keywords in your headings and subheadings. Use them in the first and last paragraphs on the page. Use them as the anchor text for links. For example, instead of creating a link on the phrase "Click here," link to "Register now for the conference." The anchor text in both your links and your navigational menus is very important to the search engines.

Page Titles and Tags

The title of each page on your site (what appears in the title bar of your web browser) should also contain keywords, as should the heading tags. This may be something your webmaster has to take care of.

Page URLs or Permalinks

If you have control over what appears in the actual URL for the page, put keywords there too. A URL like studies.htm tells the search engines very little, but one like early-child-education-impact-studies.htm says so much more. Again, your webmaster may need to help with this one.

Label Your Images

A photo called dogsreadyforadoption.jpg is more meaningful to search engines than image1234.jpg. Also, use the alt text to give the image a label, like "These dogs are now available for adoption." Not only will this help the search engines, but it's also required if you want your site to be useful to those with visual impairments and to people surfing your site on smartphones that don't load HTML and images.

Use Animation Sparingly

The search engines can't read Flash animation and can only read the tags on images and videos. It's fine to use these elements on your site, but make sure that you also have plenty of text on the page. Avoid those Flash intro pages entirely.

Search engines can't read them, and most people click through them to get to the real content anyway.

Beg, Barter, Buy, and Bait Links

Incoming links to your website from other reputable and related websites and blogs provide one of the best ways to improve your search engine rankings. You can beg for links, which is simply asking other people to link to your site. You can barter for links, which is offering something in exchange for a link, such as a reciprocal link on your site. Beware of link farms (sites with nothing but link after link instead of real content), however. All links are not created equal. Don't link with unrelated or disreputable sites just to get a link to your site.

You can buy small ads that contain your links through advertising programs like Google Adwords, which displays ads next to search results and on the websites of businesses and organizations that have agreed to display ads on their sites through the Google AdSense program. As a nonprofit, rather than paying for your ads to appear, you can apply for a Google Grant to get free advertising credits from Google.

Finally, and best of all, you can bait links, which means producing content that is so good that others can't help but link to it and pass the links on to their friends through social media sites like Facebook and Twitter.

ESTABLISH YOUR SOCIAL MEDIA PRESENCE

Social media isn't a fad for the young. It's a revolution in the way people not only use the Internet but also connect with other human beings across the street and around the planet. It's here to stay. No one can say for sure how long services popular when this book was published—like Facebook, Twitter, YouTube, and Flickr—will be around, but the concept of social media—allowing people not only to create content, but to share it, talk about it, and remix it—is here to stay. Having a presence in at least one social space is rapidly becoming a basic requirement for nonprofits, along with having your own website. Select one social media or social networking site where your supporters are already gathering and commit to participating in an existing community or building a new one there. Start conversations, respond to questions, and thank people for their interest and support.

Which site you choose depends on your audience and the type of work you do. If you take a visual approach to your marketing, then a photo site like Flickr or a video site like YouTube, Vimeo, or Blip.tv will make sense. If you work in a field where things change rapidly or you need to mobilize people quickly, Twitter makes more sense. For most nonprofits, creating a page on Facebook is probably the best default entry to the social media space.

GIVE NEW CONTACTS MULTIPLE OPTIONS FOR STAYING IN TOUCH

Once a potential new supporter finds you through your home base, your website, social media, or some other venue, you need to offer at least one way for that person to connect with your organization so that you can stay in touch.

If they first found you online, they may provide you with only an email address. If they registered for an in-person event, you may have only a snail mail address, and that's fine. Many people will be reluctant to share all of their contact information with you until they trust that you won't abuse that information. Over time, try to develop a more complete contact profile for your supporters so you can contact them through multiple channels. It's extremely important that your contact with supporters be permission-based. In other words, they have indicated that they want to receive information from you and have given you permission to contact them.

If you are using online marketing, there are three ways for you and your supporters to stay in touch with each other: email, RSS feeds, and personal "streams" or "feeds" associated with social networking profiles.

GROW YOUR EMAIL LIST

The best way to communicate directly with your supporters online is through email, especially if you plan to fundraise online. Three-quarters of the money raised online by Barack Obama's presidential campaign was directly attributable to an email solicitation, reports Colin Delany of epolitics.com. Email marketing allows you to segment your lists into different groups, to personalize each email with the supporter's name, and to track who opens your email and what links they click on.

List churn—that is, the drop in your email list size as people change email addresses without telling you or unsubscribe from your list—is inevitable. Many nonprofits lose 20 to 30 percent of their lists each year to this natural turnover.

Building an email list from scratch—and growing it to compensate for the inevitable list churn—can be a challenge.

Easy ways to build an email list include putting the e-newsletter sign-up box in your website template so it appears on every page of your site and requesting email addresses on every form you ask people to complete. But you can grow your list much more quickly if you also use the following approaches:

- *Entice readers with promised benefits—and deliver.* Email addresses are valuable. What are you giving your supporter in exchange for that valuable email address? Don't just say, "We want to send you a newsletter." Explain what kind of interesting, exclusive, and timely information your supporters will receive from you in that newsletter.
- *Collect email addresses offline.* Don't get stuck in the single-channel mindset. When you see supporters in person, ask for their email addresses. Bring a paper sign-up sheet to your events and leave one on your reception desk. Fill in the gaps by calling supporters and asking for permission to email them.
- *Make changing an email address easy.* Ideally, subscribers to your newsletter should be able to update their own email addresses with just a few clicks. The harder you make it (for example, forcing them to unsubscribe and resubscribe), the more likely they are to drop off your list for good.
- *Offer a special download.* If many people approach your organization with the same kinds of questions, create a guide or white paper with the answers. Explain clearly that when they register for the free download, they'll also be added to your e-newsletter list.
- *Put their privacy concerns to rest.* Many people assume that when they give their email address to a nonprofit, the organization will sell or rent it to other causes, creating an unwanted flood of spam. Put your supporters at ease by assuring them that you will not rent, sell, or otherwise share their email addresses with others (and then don't!).

The Palm Beach Opera used a variety of approaches to revive an ailing email list of nine hundred email addresses, most of which were invalid, says Ceci Dadisman, group sales and e-marketing manager for the Palm Beach Opera. "We started to actively collect email addresses via paper forms, such as subscription renewals and donation forms and asking over the phone during every ticket or donation transaction. We also put a link to sign up for our e-communications on each page of our website," says Ceci. "We now have over seven thousand email addresses that are divided up into highly segmented lists, and our open rates have skyrocketed."

No matter which tactics you use to build your list, you should always make it clear that unsubscribing will be painless and that you will not sell subscriber addresses to anyone else. That's the best way to establish the trust you'll need to succeed with your email marketing campaigns.

GROW YOUR LIST OF RSS SUBSCRIBERS

Offering RSS feeds and growing your list of subscribers to them is another way to connect with your supporters online.

RSS (Real Simple Syndication) feeds allow people to subscribe to the new content you create, much like they subscribe to a magazine. When you publish content—usually through a blog, podcast, or video channel—subscribers to your RSS feed get that information sent to them automatically. You don't have to send it to them yourself; it's automatically sent to your subscribers after you publish your blog post or podcast.

Subscribers then view the content in your RSS feed either through a feed reader, like Google Reader, or through another program that gathers feeds for them, such as iTunes for podcasts. People can often subscribe to RSS feeds via email too, which means that your new blog post would automatically be emailed to the subscriber instead of appearing in their feed reader.

So, should you start a blog? I'm a big advocate of blogging for nonprofits because it's an easy, convenient way to share your stories with supporters. Blogs can also help boost your search engine rankings. But they aren't for everyone.

To help you think through this question, here are my top five reasons why a nonprofit should have a blog and my top five reasons why a nonprofit shouldn't.

You *Do* Need a Blog If . . .

1. *You need a better way to share the small stuff.* You have many wonderful little anecdotes that your supporters would love to hear. You also run across cool resources and surprising statistics all the time, but none of it really ranks as "newsletter worthy" because they are too short. Blogs are perfect for fifty-word updates.

2. *You need to take people behind the scenes.* This is especially important for organizations that work in places people either can't get to easily on their own (for example, overseas or restricted areas like hospital wards or prisons) or are reluctant to visit, even if they could (for example, the "bad part of town"). For your supporters to really get what you do, they have to understand where you do it. Blogging lets you take them there by giving you a platform to share stories and photos over time, creating an ongoing narrative, post by post, all in one easily accessible place.

3. *You need a better way to organize the resources you have available.* If you see yourself as a service, training, or resource provider, you probably have a ton of information on your website that is actually pretty tough for people to find. One of the beautiful things about blogging is that categories and tags are a natural part of the software, so you can easily group items and your readers can easily find them.

4. *You need to react quickly.* If your organization responds to breaking news, I don't see how you can be effective online without a blog—or without the functional equivalent built into your website (namely, some other kind of RSS-producing "news" section).

5. *You need to incubate content for bigger publications.* If you produce reports, white papers, books, and the like, then a blog is perfect for your organization. It lets you publish bits and pieces as you create them and get comments from others who care about your issues. Then it's all right there when you are ready to create a larger publication.

You *Don't* Need a Blog If . . .

1. *Transparency is too scary.* Blogging is about sharing. If the idea of strangers getting a peek into your work makes you extremely nervous, then forget about blogging.

2. *Writing in a personal tone of voice is too hard.* Good blog writing is direct, conversational, and personal. If you are only comfortable writing as "the organization" rather than as a person working at the organization, then blogging is not for you.

3. *Criticism is too scary.* If you only want to hear from people who agree with you, blogging is not for you. In my opinion, you can't turn off comments and

still call what you are doing blogging. Yes, you need to moderate the incoming comments, but don't delete comments just because they are critical.

4. *You can't make the time.* Because of the chronological nature of blogging, people pay attention to how often you post. If you can't post at least once a week, blogging probably isn't for you.
5. *You can't articulate the value of your blog.* If you don't know how your blog fits into your nonprofit marketing strategy and what you want to accomplish with it, then don't do it.

GROW YOUR LIST OF FRIENDS AND FOLLOWERS

Social networking sites allow individuals to connect to other individuals and to organizations by becoming friends, fans, or followers (the lexicon varies based on the site). When you add something to your profile on a social networking site, such as updating your status on Facebook or tweeting on Twitter, whatever you post is sent out to your contacts on that site. This flow of information from you to your friends, fans, or followers is often called your "stream" or "feed." Social networking sites make it easy for friends of friends to see and share information, which spreads your updates even further. Table 8.1 sorts out the different names for these contacts on the various sites.

Table 8.1.
What to Call Your Online Contacts in Social Networking Sites

Blogs	Individuals become *subscribers* of the blog when they sign up to receive the RSS feed.
Facebook	Individuals become *friends* with each other via personal profiles.
	Individuals become a *fan* of an organization's or celebrity's Facebook page.
	Individuals become *members* of a nonprofit's Facebook cause.
	Individuals become *members* of a Facebook group.
Twitter	Individuals become *followers* of other Twitter users.
YouTube	Individuals become *subscribers* to a video channel and can also be a *friend* of other YouTube users.

No matter which channels you use, always work on keeping your lists of supporters healthy and growing. You'll find more tips on building your lists of online supporters on the companion website.

STAY CONSISTENT: BRANDING YOUR NONPROFIT

When you are trying to be visible in multiple places and to communicate with participants and supporters in various ways, it's easy to end up with a mishmash of ways your organization is represented, both in print and online. What someone sees in an advertisement may be so different from what they see on your website that they don't realize it's all from the same organization, which defeats the purpose of marketing in the first place.

Nancy Schwartz of GettingAttention.org suggests the following four-step plan to keep your brand consistent across multiple channels.[2]

1. *Make sure that there's agreement, within leadership and key departmental staff, on what your brand is.* The brand portfolio includes your positioning statement, key messages for your organization and for each of your programs or services, and design guidelines on use of your logo and colors. Brand consists of the core marketing elements (both graphic and narrative) that, when used consistently, ensure that your nonprofit is quickly recognized and understood by your key audiences. Every nonprofit needs a strong brand.

2. *Create a process for creation and review of marketing materials.* Discuss the communications creation process with your colleagues and, with input from representative staff departments, create a process for creation and review of marketing materials. Discuss what happens before and after materials come through your organization's communications staff (or whoever has responsibility for development and approval of communications materials).

3. *Design and implement tools to make it easier for colleagues to develop or generate communications that convey the brand.* Select a standard style guide (*Chicago Manual of Style*, *Words into Type*, or *AP Stylebook*) and dictionary as your standards. Create a custom style guide as needed. Create templates (in Microsoft Word or another word processing program used by staff) for the most common communications materials. These may include a one-page flyer, a tri-panel brochure on services, and a press release. Make these available for download so

that your colleagues have a quick-and-dirty way of creating communications that are aligned with your brand.

4. *Hold a training session.* Here you can explain what the brand is (messages, design standards, style guide, processes, and templates) and why it's important to be consistent in using it. Include scenarios to illustrate how the communications creations process works, rather than just distributing the guide.

CONCLUSION: DON'T LET POTENTIAL SUPPORTERS SLIP AWAY

According to Convio's Online Marketing Nonprofit Benchmark Index Study, only 3 percent—3 percent!—of monthly visitors to nonprofit websites provide their email address to the organization by registering for email updates or taking some other action online. This rate hasn't changed much from 2007–2009. The remaining 97 percent of visitors to nonprofit websites either have registered earlier (probably a very small percentage, representing frequent repeat visitors) or represent a huge opportunity to move beyond merely being found by a potential supporter online to making that connection that allows a conversation to begin. Be visible, and when those people find you, don't let them slip away. Offer them an easy, meaningful way to connect.

chapter NINE

Become an Expert Source for the Media and Decision Makers

To be trusted is a greater compliment than to be loved.

—George Macdonald

This chapter is about . . .

- **Positioning your nonprofit as an expert source**
- **Strategies to raise your profile as an expert**
- **How to pitch a story to the media**

You believe that your program to keep teenagers from dropping out of school is one of the most innovative and effective around, yet you can't get any press coverage. No matter how many press releases and newsletters you send out, it's always the school district officials, PTA leaders, and other nonprofits running after-school programs that get called for media interviews, or asked to testify at legislative committee hearings, or invited to speak at professional conferences.

Why, your board president asks, aren't you the one they call? After all, media coverage is one important way for potential new clients, participants, supporters, partners, and donors to learn about your organization. When you appear in respected publications produced by others, some of that respect rubs off on you in the readers' or viewers' eyes (assuming the mention was positive, of course).

Some people would answer the board president's question defensively and blame the reporters for not doing a thorough job researching who's really doing what in the community. Others might respond with jealousy and try to discredit the contributions of the other groups who are getting all the attention. Still others would shrug, completely mystified by how these organizations manage to get so much attention from the news media.

WHY SOME GROUPS GET THE CALL AND OTHERS DON'T

The groups that get the call are perceived as *expert sources.* Nonprofits that are viewed as experts by the media, decision makers, and their professional colleagues may reach the top of the call list through some intangibles like finesse, luck, and personality. But they get there primarily through hard work.

Being viewed as an expert source is a great nonprofit marketing strategy because it can produce lots of publicity. Other people, nonprofits, and media outlets—often with greater influence and reach than your organization—write and talk about you. Unlike advertising or marketing communications that you create and distribute yourself, this is publicity you don't have to pay for!

The nonprofit sector as a whole is well positioned to be considered a source of expertise by the media, policymakers, and the public for several reasons. First, a certain level of purity is associated with the nonprofit sector. You're supposed to be nonpartisan. You're supposed to have a social or civic-minded purpose. Nearly all nonprofits have a mission that is easily tied to a public benefit rather than to personal glory or money. That altruism makes you trustworthy.

The nonprofit sector as a whole is generally not considered to be very powerful. In recent polls, Americans say they would actually like to see nonprofits have more power and more decision-making authority in our society. Power is often seen as a corrupting influence, and because people consider nonprofits to be one of the less powerful sectors of society, being part of it increases your credibility.

Also, you are doing interesting work. You're helping real people with real problems. Nonprofits have great anecdotes and access to people with amazing personal stories related to all of the hot issues of the day. The media loves a good story, and nonprofits have both stories to tell and access to plenty of people to interview.

But being a nonprofit alone won't position you as an expert source. You can't wait on the sidelines assuming people will call you. You have to get up off the bench and into the game, first by understanding the five qualities of a good expert source and then by pursuing seven strategies that raise your visibility as an expert.

THE FIVE QUALITIES OF A GOOD EXPERT SOURCE

To be a good expert source, you have to embody five qualities. You need to be accessible, cooperative, and trustworthy, and you need a well-understood niche and solid track record.

Be Accessible

The first and most important quality of an expert source for the news media is being accessible. A reporter or an editor on deadline will always pick the person she can reach quickly over the smartest person who's nearly impossible to get ahold of, especially on nights and weekends. You may be the best source on paper—you may have the best quotes and the best information—but if journalists can't reach you when the deadline clock is ticking down, they will run that story without you.

Make getting in touch with you easy by publishing several different ways to contact you, including off-hours phone numbers, on your website. If you are serious about wanting more press coverage, then you need to make your cell phone number publicly available. If you don't have a cell phone, consider publishing your home phone number as well. If you aren't comfortable listing these numbers online, then include them in your voice mail greeting on your office line.

The same goes for your email address. Some organizations try to mask email addresses from website spammers by using web contact forms instead. But reporters don't want to use a web form; they want to reach you, the expert, directly. Rather than hiding your email address from people whom you really do want to hear from, set up a good spam filter instead.

Be prepared to take phone calls in the evenings and on weekends. Media deadlines are often outside the typical 9:00 AM to 5:00 PM, Monday through Friday schedule. That doesn't mean you have to take a reporter's call immediately and spend a half-hour answering questions during family dinner time. But it does mean that you should return voicemails promptly. If you do answer the call, it's fine to ask whether the reporter is on deadline and to schedule a better time to talk, whether it's in thirty minutes or the next day.

Be Cooperative

When someone calls a person they expect to be an expert, they are looking for the "Bingo!" moment. That's when you give them something they are looking for, perhaps an interesting story, a surprising statistic, and an intriguing quote. Whatever it is, in their own minds, as you are speaking, they think, "Bingo! That's just what I needed! I called the right person!"

You get to the "Bingo!" moment by listening. Let your callers set the agenda. They are calling you because they have specific questions, or they have a particular angle that they're working. Even if you think the caller is asking a really dumb or irrelevant question, answer it. If you don't answer their questions first, you will be seen as uncooperative and likely won't be called again.

Focus on what they're interested in, at least at first. Once you've answered those initial questions, you can start to steer the conversation in another direction. You might say, "Did you know . . . ?" or "Have you thought about . . . ?" You can lead the caller down another path that you think is more interesting or newsworthy.

Reporters in particular also love brief, but substantive answers. Although it can be difficult to do without practice, try to talk in bullet points or sound bites. Part of being an expert is anticipating the kinds of questions people have about your topic, and knowing your talking points so well that they smoothly roll off your tongue, no matter how much you may be caught off guard when the call comes in. Give reporters those nuggets of information and those short quotable quotes, in plain English. You won't find jargon in the newspaper or on TV, so don't use it in an interview with a reporter. The only exception would be with writers for trade press magazines who are familiar with your lingo. They can use it, because their readers know it and use it too.

Being cooperative also means being resourceful for whoever is calling on you as the expert. Offer other sources of information. Give them other experts' names and phone numbers and email addresses. Be as helpful as you can in identifying people for the "man on the street" perspective. Turn them onto really good websites where they can find some good background information or statistics for the story.

Own a Well-Understood Niche

You don't know everything. No one does. So don't pretend that you do. Instead, narrow down the areas that you want to be known for. What is your little piece of the larger pie of expertise in your field? How is your particular perspective different from those of other experts?

Let's say you work in animal rights, and a reporter is working on a story about how animals are treated in circuses and water parks. That reporter will want to talk to somebody who knows about wild animals in captivity. They will not be interested in talking to an animal rights advocate who spends most of her time on issues that affect cats and dogs.

In this case, putting yourself out there as an advocate for animals is not going to be enough to put you on that reporter's call list, even if she does know who you are. Your area of expertise is too broad. Instead, you need to narrow it down and put yourself out there as an expert on specific issues, such as how elephants or dolphins behave in entertainment venues.

Once you narrow down your niche, you want other experts in your larger field to recognize your expertise so that they can refer misdirected calls they receive to you. In our example, you might professionally befriend animal experts who deal with factory farming issues. If you get calls about pigs and cows, you can pass on their contact information. If they get calls about the circus, they can refer them to you. Home in on what you are good at, what you know a lot about, and where you have bountiful resources to fall back on if you can't answer the caller's questions.

Build a Solid Track Record

The more often you are quoted, the more likely others will call you. But even without a solid track record, you can still establish some credibility, starting with your job title. Executive directors are more likely to be quoted than executive assistants. If you don't have a decent title, play up your experience instead. Create a short tagline for yourself that quickly explains why you would make a great source:

- Twenty years of experience living and working with the homeless
- Raised $5 million to provide low-income children with health care
- Managed a spay-neuter program that treated seven hundred cats and dogs in one summer

In addition to being cooperative, being consistent will also add to your track record. You want to be known for talking intelligently about your issues. You want to be known for returning phone calls and emails promptly. You want to be known for giving the good quotes. You want to be known for a wide-ranging network of people and giving good referrals. Even when you don't know the answers yourself, you can build your track record as a great expert source simply by knowing where else to go for the information.

Be Trustworthy

The fifth quality of a great expert source is being trustworthy. According to a Harris Interactive poll from August 2006, the most trusted professionals are doctors, teachers, scientists, police officers, and professors. Conversely, some of the least trusted are actors, lawyers, stockbrokers, trade union leaders, and opinion pollsters.

What's the difference? The most trusted group of professionals helps people, saves lives, and values training and objectivity. They don't have a particular vested interest, and they tend to stay out of the fray. The least trusted group, on the other hand, is often considered disingenuous, shallow, and greedy.

Now let's look at which nonprofit organizations working inside the Beltway in Washington, D.C., the public trusts and doesn't trust, based on another Harris Interactive poll from December 2008. Consumer Reports, American Red Cross, AARP, and the Nature Conservancy all rated very highly as trusted nonprofit organizations. Unions, the American Civil Liberties Union, the National Rifle Association, and PhRMA (the Pharmaceutical Research and Manufacturers of America) were the least trusted.

Just as we saw with the survey on professional trustworthiness, groups that are considered to be working for the larger good are trusted far more than those who are outspoken advocates of relatively narrow points of view or special interests. It's also worth noting that the same poll about trust also asked about power, and the lists flip-flopped, with the most trustworthy groups considered to be the least powerful and the least trustworthy groups considered the most powerful.

So how can your nonprofit be a strong advocate for your cause, be politically powerful, and still remain trustworthy in the eyes of the public? It's all about transparency. You are what you are, and you should be completely honest and confident about it. There's no pretense in your communications and no hidden agendas in your marketing. You remain true to your public mission as a nonprofit and recognize opposing views with respect.

SEVEN STRATEGIES TO RAISE YOUR PROFILE AS AN EXPERT SOURCE

Now that you understand what people are looking for in an expert source and you are working to embody these five qualities, how do you go about raising your visibility so people know you exist and how to reach you? Work through the following seven strategies.

Pass the Background Check

People want to check you out before they call you. This is true for reporters, publishers, conference organizers, and anyone else who is thinking about asking for your expertise. Google is the background checker of choice when people are looking for expert sources, which means you need a good website.

On your website, you should have a basic online press kit. Include a short, simple explanation of what your organization does, for whom, and why. Include some good stories that demonstrate both the need for your organization and your successes. Add links to other articles, both those that have quoted you and those you have written yourself. You might also include statistics relevant to your cause and frequently asked questions (FAQ).

Include short bios for key staff members, with photos, that include both professional credentials and some personal details as well, so we see them as real human beings. Add contact information next to each name.

Work the Word of Mouth

Testimonials from others about how helpful, insightful, and smart the people in your organization are will go a long way in generating more calls for your expertise. Gather these short quotes from surveys, comment forms, your email box, and anywhere else you find people saying nice things about you and your work. It's best to use the person's name, so ask permission to include the testimonial on your website. If obtaining permission is impractical or impossible (for example, taking comments from anonymous evaluation forms where you spoke at a conference), simply list the person's relationship to you (for example, annual conference attendee).

Just as you want others to be generous with their praise of and referrals to you, you need to be equally generous in talking about the good works and expertise of others. Remember, you are focusing on one particular piece of the pie as your expertise. Be friendly with people claiming those other pieces of pie that are not as important to you. Lavish praise on them, and they'll notice you and remember you the next time someone calls them looking for your kind of expertise.

Nurture Big Brains and Big Mouths

If your organization's staff includes grand thinkers and great talkers, capitalize on that. Get out there and let people know what you're thinking and share those opinions. Big ideas and big opinions get people excited and generate headlines. Nonprofits with organizational personalities that are like the wallflower at the school dance will have a harder time being recognized as an expert than groups that are the life of the party.

If you don't have those big brains and big mouths on staff, then create some partnerships with others who do. Seek out academics, independent consultants, or authors who believe in your cause and your work but are better spokespeople than your staff members. Give them a title, even if the position is unpaid. Your organization becomes, in effect, their public voice and, they become your expert source for the media. You work together to raise both of your profiles.

Publish Constantly

Most highly visible experts are publishing constantly. Although books are still great credibility boosters, they are very time-consuming to produce. To more quickly raise your visibility and improve your search engine rankings at the same time, publish online instead. Online publishing through websites, blogs, email newsletters, and podcasts is both fast and affordable.

Write an e-book or white paper that people can download for free from your website. Publish case studies, Q &A interviews, and how-to articles on your website. Blog about your work, providing a behind-the-scenes perspective. Write articles for association newsletters. Record yourself speaking about a topic and offer it as a podcast.

But don't publish about just anything. Remember, you want to build your reputation within your particular niche. Be strategic about how much you publish on various topics.

Listen for Opportunities to Speak Up

Listen for opportunities to share your expertise at all times. Chapter Three discusses many different techniques for listening, including Google Alerts, searches delivered to you via RSS, and monitoring services.

You can also participate in services created especially to connect expert sources and journalists. Help a Reporter Out (HARO) is a free service that compiles requests for sources from journalists and emails them to experts daily. PR Newswire runs Profnet, a paid media contact service.

When using services like these, it is essential that you respond only when your expertise matches well what the journalist is requesting. Off-topic and "I just wanted to introduce myself" responses to the specific inquiries posted through these services are not appreciated.

Answer Questions

Of course, journalists aren't the only ones seeking experts. Other professionals and the public are doing the same thing for their own needs.

LinkedIn Answers is a service on the business networking site LinkedIn. Users can post questions, which are organized by categories, including a nonprofit section. You and several other people will typically answer a question and the person who posted it can vote on the best answer. If you post enough best answers, LinkedIn will identify you as an expert in that category. Yahoo! Answers is a similar program for more consumer-oriented questions.

Most social networking sites also allow the creation of special groups; for example, on Facebook Groups, members will post questions on particular topics that you can answer. Message board and email discussion lists like Google Groups and Yahoo! Groups are also full of questions awaiting expert answers.

You can also answer questions on your own website by setting up a FAQ page where visitors can submit questions or by holding online office hours in which you use a chat or instant messaging service to communicate with visitors in real time.

Teach Courses

Look into opportunities to share your expertise specifically with people who are seeking education on your topics. You can pursue formal teaching opportunities at local colleges and universities, including professional certificate programs. You can teach through associations, especially those that offer certifications that require continuing education credits. You can also set up your own workshops or webinars to share what you know and teach others how to complete those tasks at which you excel.

HOW TO PITCH YOUR STORY TO THE MEDIA

If you've never called a reporter to pitch a story before, relax. It's not that hard, if you follow these tips.

Skip the "blanket pitch." Don't contact every single reporter you can think of with the same pitch. It doesn't work. You have to personalize for each reporter.

Know your "newsy" hook. Is your story timely or unusual? Will it impact many people or does it involve a prominent person? Does it have a compelling human interest angle? Study the kinds of articles and broadcasts produced by the media outlets you are calling to get a sense for what they consider newsy.

Know your angle with each particular reporter. Sometimes you end up calling a general assignment reporter, and that's fine. You can go with a more straightforward pitch. But if you want your story in the business section, you need to pitch a business reporter, and your story should have a clear business angle. Nonprofit events could appear in virtually every section of the paper with the right angle and press release content (include quotes from elected officials if you are trying for the "Local" section or talking to the government beat reporter, quotes from business leaders if you are trying for the business section, and so on).

Connect your pitch to past reporting, if you can. If the reporter has previously written about your topic or organization, definitely mention that (for example: "You wrote a great story about this in May, and I think this would be an excellent follow-up . . .").

Offer more than a press release. Will there be good photo opportunities? Can you put the reporter in touch with several people to interview? Any behind-the-scenes tours of particularly interesting or exclusive venues or backstage interviews with big keynote speakers or high-profile guests?

Practice your pitch. Practice getting your pitch down to thirty seconds, with the most important information in your first sentence. Most reporters will have no problem interrupting you and telling you they aren't interested if you don't grab them fast. You'll hear something like "It's not right for us," "Timing isn't good," a flat out "No thanks," or "I don't know; I'll call you back"—which usually means no.

Don't get defensive or abusive if the reporter says no. Don't insult the reporter by saying things like, "Wow, you really don't get it" or "You are really missing out on the biggest story of the year." Reporters know better than you what they cover; if it really is the biggest story of the year, and the reporter turns it down, it's because your pitch is no good.

Here's a sample pitch.

Reporter

John Smith: Hello, John Smith.

You: Hi, John. My name is Bob Evans with Save the Squirrels. I have a story for you. [Note, you aren't saying, "I have the best story ever" or "a story you'd be an idiot to pass up"—keep it as a straightforward suggestion.]

or

You: Hi, John. My name is Bob Evans with Save the Squirrels. I'd like to pitch a story to you really quickly if you have a minute. [Yes, it's OK to call what you are doing pitching. That's the term for it. The reporters know that's what you are doing, so it's no big deal to say it.]

Reporter: You've caught me at a bad time; I'm right in the middle of something . . . [But he doesn't blow you off entirely.]

You: I'll make it really quick, I promise . . .

or

Reporter: OK, go ahead.

You: [Launch right into it! No need for small talk or a bunch of background; just get to the point.] Our local squirrel population has been decimated, and on Saturday we are holding a special Dog Walk and Festival at City Park to raise money for a breeding program. Dogs love to chase squirrels, and dog owners all over town are reporting high levels of depression since the dogs have nothing to chase now. We are expecting at least a hundred people and dogs at the festival, and we'll have all kinds of fun contests, including a Dog/Owner Look-Alike Contest and an *American Idol*-style howling contest where the fire department will sound the truck sirens to get the dogs going. It's going to be lots of fun, with great photo opps, and all of the money will go directly to solving our local squirrel problem.

Reporter: Do you have any numbers on the problem?

You: Yes, a university study showed that our squirrel population is down by 50 percent.

Reporter:	How do we know the dogs are depressed?
You:	Dog owners can tell, and vets across town are being asked for antidepressants.
Reporter:	Any vets actually giving out the pills?
You:	Yeah, I can put you in touch with one or two. Do you want me to email you the press release for the festival and some vet contacts?
Reporter:	Sure. I'll see what I can do.
You:	Thanks, John. Let me give you my cell phone number . . .

It's really that simple. But notice how the reporter went off on a tangent with the dog depression rather than focusing on the Dog Walk and Festival? This happens all the time! Keep in mind that reporters decide what the story really is. You can always try to steer them back to your angle, but ultimately the reporters will decide what to write about or whether to cover it at all.

Respect that, and don't get pushy or critical about their decisions. A story about vets prescribing antidepressants that mentions your festival is better than no story at all! And now you know the reporter a little better and can come back next time with an even more focused pitch for John Smith.

Reporters tend to be skeptical by nature, so don't be put off if one quizzes you or don't seem particularly excited. Work your pitch, and follow up with whatever the reporter asks for. Remember, you need each other. Reporters need good stories, and you need the publicity. Build those relationships, give reporters what they need (good stories!), and you'll get some great press in return.

WHO IS THE EXPERT? YOU OR THE ORGANIZATION?

Before you launch a publicity campaign using these strategies to raise your visibility as an expert, it's important to distinguish between marketing your nonprofit as the expert and marketing individual staff members as experts. Although you can do both, you should be clear about your intentions from the start.

Many times it will make sense for a nonprofit to identify just one or two people as their primary spokespeople, and this is often determined by job description. Even if you are promoting the organization as the expert, it's only natural that some people will associate that expertise with the person instead. If one of those people moves on to another job, they may or may not take some of the credibility with them.

Be up front in your staff discussions about marketing your experts, and you can avoid any uncomfortable feelings later about personal agendas and career advancement.

CONCLUSION: CREATE SOMETHING NEW AND SHARE IT

You can't become the kind of expert that others want to quote without doing the hard work to create that expertise. For many organizations, this means performing original research or analyzing data generated by others in innovative ways. That means you are building time into the life of your nonprofit to do your homework, to think about issues and approaches, and to share what you have learned. Hoarding information and ideas and then expecting others to clamor around your feet for words of wisdom simply doesn't work anymore; there are too many other experts—self-described or otherwise—right around the corner or a simple Google search away who are willing to give away what they know for free.

Find your niche. Work hard to create something new. Have something interesting to say. Then share it with others. That's how you become known as an expert source.

chapter **TEN**

Stay in Touch with Your Community of Supporters

The way we communicate with others and with ourselves ultimately determines the quality of our lives.

—Anthony Robbins

This chapter is about . . .

- Thinking of your organization as a media mogul
- Creating and sending regular and frequent communications to supporters
- Using a content creation strategy and editorial calendar to manage the production of your communications
- Communicating through social media conversations

Once you've connected with a potential supporter and you have at least one way to stay in touch, you need to start a conversation with that person. Only by keeping the lines of communication open in both directions will you turn that initial interest in your cause into a long-term commitment to it. In fact, this is absolutely essential if you eventually plan to ask this new supporter for money. As Penelope Burk says in her must-read *Donor-Centered Fundraising,*

"Meaningful information on their gifts at work is the key to donors' repeat and increased giving. Communication is the process by which information is delivered. Fundraising under-performance, therefore, is actually a failure to communicate."

Your job now, regardless of whether you consider new contacts to be fundraising prospects or not, is to educate, to pique their interest in what's possible, and to inspire them to help you achieve your mission. To build that kind of relationship over time, you need to communicate regularly. On a very practical level, you need to take into account the kind of information that your new and current supporters want to receive from you and how often and in what formats they prefer to receive it. Likewise, you need to consider your capacity to meet those expectations.

THINK OF YOUR ORGANIZATION AS A MEDIA MOGUL

Everyone is a publisher. Everyone is a broadcaster. Everyone, including your nonprofit, can be a media mogul, thanks to Web 2.0. Nonprofits are no longer dependent on the media to get their messages out beyond their inner circles, yet so many groups are still fretting about whether to double-space a press release. Traditional media still plays an important role, but it's not what it used to be.

Instead of visualizing an article about your cause in thousands of newspapers landing in the driveways of your potential supporters, you should be looking at ways to generate thousands of messages from members of your inner circle to their own inner circles, talking about your cause, using everything from email to social media to do it. The tools to make that happen are now easy and inexpensive.

Start by creating a good website and establishing a solid email marketing program. Do not move forward until these two essential elements of your online media empire are in place. They do not need to be perfect. Presentable works in progress are completely acceptable.

Next, start venturing out into social media, which could include blogging, podcasting, videos, and social networking sites like Facebook, Twitter, and literally hundreds of other social media opportunities. Play around and experiment with personal profiles, listening all the while, until you have a good sense for where your nonprofit should start. Select one or two social media sites or elements (like a blog or message board on your site), do those well, then expand from there.

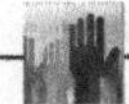

UNFAMILIAR WITH SOME OF THE TERMS IN THIS CHAPTER?

If you find some of the terminology in this section foreign or confusing, refer to the Glossary of Online Marketing Terms at the back of the book.

STRIVE FOR SHORTER, MORE FREQUENT COMMUNICATIONS IN MULTIPLE PLACES

Research on what donors really want from the nonprofits they support shows that your typical twelve-page print newsletter is not the best way to stay in touch. In *Donor-Centered Fundraising*, Penelope Burk reports that 88 percent of the nonprofits she surveyed publish a print newsletter and 59 percent of them produce newsletters that are eight pages or longer. Yet 66 percent of the donors in her study said they don't have time to read charity newsletters thoroughly, and 58 percent said that nonprofit newsletters are too long. In fact, Burk reports that 65 percent of individual donors and 87 percent of corporate donors would prefer a one-page update or bulletin instead.

If a long printed quarterly newsletter isn't what donors want, then what is? The answer for your nonprofit lies in knowing your supporters and asking them what they'd like. But think about how you stay in touch with good friends who don't live close by. Although they may send you a long Christmas letter (the personal friend version of a nonprofit's annual report), they don't send you a twelve-page newsletter every three months and never talk to you otherwise. They send you shorter, more frequent updates through phone calls, email messages, the occasional greeting card, and updates on social networking sites where you've connected. They ask you questions about how you are doing too. Take the same approach with your nonprofit's supporters.

You also need to understand for yourself what your organization can reasonably expect to produce on a regular schedule given your resource constraints. So much of successful nonprofit marketing depends on the creation of great content, including articles for your newsletter, website, blog, press releases, and so on, as well as images and video. How much great content do you think you can create and how often? How much you communicate, when, and where is the product of both elements: what they want and what you can realistically produce.

If you don't know where to begin, I suggest that you contact your supporters an average of once a month, whether by direct mail letter, a one- or two-page printed newsletter, an email newsletter, or a combination. If your fundraising and marketing departments send separate communications to the same list, you need to work together to coordinate your schedules—it's all communication from the same place as far as your supporters are concerned.

Although I recommend monthly contact as a starting point, you don't need to force yourself into a strict publishing schedule. You shouldn't send a newsletter just because your editorial calendar tells you to. You need to have good, timely content to share with your supporters. Let the content drive the schedule. If your newsletters are three weeks apart and then six weeks apart, that's fine, as long as the content is timely and interesting. If you don't have something interesting to say to your supporters once a month on average, you probably need to start thinking more creatively about ways to tell your story.

This once-a-month goal does not include any contacts through social media like a blog or a Facebook or Twitter account, which have their own user cultures, with community expectations varying from platform to platform. Again, how often you need to update depends entirely on how you are using these tools in your marketing strategy and what expectations you have set with your blog subscribers, Facebook fans, Twitter followers, and other online friends. If you are starting from scratch and don't know where to begin, I'd advise you to update your blog at least once a week, your Facebook page or profile at least two or three times per week, and a Twitter account several times a week, if not daily.

All of these time frames are defaults that you need to tweak to your particular situation. See how it goes and what kind of response you get. Then adjust these schedules to match what's best for your organization and your supporters.

CONSIDER THE GIFTING MODEL OF NONPROFIT COMMUNICATIONS

Think back to when you were a kid and to a time of year when you knew everyone in your family would give you presents, whether it was your birthday, Christmas, or some other special celebration. Whose gifts did you want to tear open right away, and whose were sure to disappoint?

You may recognize these five types of family gifters, if not from your own family then from all those bad holiday movies. But will you recognize your organization's approach to communications in these gifting styles? Think in particular about your newsletter, as that's the most ubiquitous form of nonprofit communication with current supporters.

Curmudgeonly Uncle

He thinks kids have it so easy these days—they're all spoiled brats who have no idea what the real world is like. To be honest, he doesn't really care what you want for your birthday, because you probably don't deserve anything anyway.

Curmudgeonly Uncle nonprofits are bitter that they have to ask for donations and report back to their supporters at all. If people don't understand their issues and support their work, it's not the nonprofit's fault. It's because the audience is full of idiots who just don't get it. In other words, nonprofit marketing is a waste of precious time they need to spend on real work, so why bother? Although I run into an organization with this attitude from time to time, thankfully they are rare, in part because once they run out of seed money, they implode.

Grandma-Knows-Best

Unlike the Curmudgeonly Uncle, Grandma-Knows-Best thinks you deserve a gift, but she doesn't really care what's on your list because she knows what's best for you. You are going to get an electric toothbrush if you are lucky, and a scarf she knitted if you aren't. Either way, that present is going to be good for you, whether you like it or not.

Grandma-Knows-Best nonprofits write newsletters full of articles about the organization, its activities, and its issues, with little regard for who actually reads the newsletter. In fact, they aren't even sure who's on the newsletter list, and it really doesn't matter. Knowing wouldn't change the content. They decide what goes into the newsletter—end of story. I'd say about a third of nonprofit newsletters fall into this category.

Slacker Brother

He knows he is supposed to get you something, but he doesn't want to put any thought or effort into it, let alone money, so he is going to regift to you something he got for his birthday.

Slacker Brother nonprofits fill their publications with articles from other sources, with little original content, because it's quick and easy and they want to check the newsletter off the to-do list. Some of it may be helpful, but it's a toss-up most of the time. About a tenth of the newsletters I see fall into this category.

Well-Meaning Mom and Dad

They know what you really want and also what you need. They give you a mix. You'll get that fun new game you wanted, because they want you to be happy, but you'll also get something they think you need, like socks and underwear.

Well-Meaning Mom and Dad nonprofits are those who are sincerely interested in understanding their audience and try to speak to their interests and values in most of their communications, but they can't quite let go of all of the organization-centered information. The boring "message from the executive director" column, for example, is still at the front of the print newsletter. Making sure that all the various programs get equal billing in the newsletter is more important to them than focusing on the programs that interest supporters the most. About half of nonprofit newsletters fall into this category.

Cool Aunt

She gets it right every time. She asks you what's on your wish list, or asks others what you are into these days. You can't wait to open her present. You'd open it the second it arrived if you could.

Cool Aunt nonprofits know who they are communicating with and are constantly checking in with their audience, whether by talking to them directly, listening through social media, or staying on top of larger trends through audience research. They regularly adjust the content of their communications, and even their publishing schedule, to be relevant to their audience right now. Their donors and supporters can tell that these nonprofits care what they think and are grateful for their participation. As much as possible, their newsletters are tools for not only delivering content but also sparking conversation and interaction. The donors and supporters love these nonprofits in return. About a tenth of the newsletters I see come from Cool Aunt organizations.

Do the print and online publications you produce and the conversations you have on social media sites feel like gifts to your participants and supporters, or are they simply what you think they need or what you want to give them for your own self-centered reasons? Start working your way down the continuum toward the Cool Aunt, and eventually you'll be the favorite nonprofit on everyone's list.

WRITE LIKE THE SMART, PASSIONATE HUMAN BEING YOU ARE (NOT THE WONKY JARGON DROID YOU SOUND LIKE NOW)

People give to and support nonprofits for highly subjective and personal reasons. Your supporters get something deeply personal out of their affiliation with your organization as a donor, volunteer, or advocate. So why would your response back to these passionate people be institutional, monolithic, and completely objective?

You need to break out of the "501(c)(3) speaks to the masses" writing mode if you want your communications to be successful. Good nonprofit writing is personal, informal, direct, friendly, and, when appropriate, funny—in other words, it's human. Although there are certainly times when the newsy, facts-only journalistic style can work, the overwhelming majority of your communications with supporters should be much friendlier. Here are a few tips:

- Speak directly to your reader by calling them "you" and refer to yourself and your nonprofit as "we" or "I."
- Use bylines. Let your readers know who is writing each article.
- Make people central to your content. Include your staff, donors, volunteers, clients, and others by name in your articles.
- Tell stories in your newsletters to engage your donors in your work, to reinforce their giving decisions, to inspire them to do more, and to encourage more word-of-mouth marketing on your behalf.
- Include headshots or photos with people. Show your readers who's talking and who you are talking about.

Your supporters give their time, talents, and gifts with passion for your cause. They are part of the family. Write to them that way.

PULL IT ALL TOGETHER WITH A CONTENT CREATION STRATEGY

You have a newsletter. You have other donor communications, like direct appeal letters and thank-you letters. You're putting together information for your specific programs, including flyers and web pages. You are communicating regularly (it may sometimes feel like *constantly*) in social media, and you are doing your best to give your participants and supporters what they want. And it's driving you crazy.

Nonprofits have always had many content buckets that need to be filled regularly. But now, with social media, it can feel like those buckets are bottomless. It can feel like you'll never have enough time to keep all of the buckets full of good content, which is especially true if you try to create original content all the time.

The soothing remedy for your content creation craziness is a content creation strategy managed through an editorial calendar. Some people suggest looking at your content creation strategy as a symphony in which all of the various pieces of content you create are the musical notes. With you as the conductor, all of these notes come together in sync to make a beautiful song: your messages getting through to your supporters and having the intended effect, whatever that may be.

But this analogy belies how messy content creation can be, especially when you are overworked and pressed for time. Rather than a well-organized, practiced, tuxedo-wearing symphony, nonprofit content creation reminds me more of a bustling kitchen of a busy family with two full-time working parents and a few always-hungry teenagers who are not unlike those bottomless buckets. Make-ahead meal planning is what keeps this family fed. The parents think about meal planning a week at a time, shop for groceries, do prep work on the weekend, and cook meals early in the week that can be reheated or remixed later in the week.

You can take the same approach with your content creation strategy. Plan ahead, get organized, and research early. Create original content with an eye for ways to remix it later. Make some content you can use now, but start baking other content for later. All people who produce content for a living, whether they be writers or musicians or artists, repurpose their content. No one produces completely original content all the time. So just how much of your content needs to be 100 percent original and fresh? And how much can be reheated or remixed? I suggest you start with a fifty-fifty balance and adjust from there. Half of what you feed to your supporters through your various channels will be brand-spanking-new content. The other half will be remixed or reheated in some way, using techniques like these.

Use a different channel. If you've written a blog post, is there something you can do with that content elsewhere? Many times your blog, your website, your email newsletter, and your print newsletter will feed each other and you'll remix between those channels. Three short blog posts can be combined into one longer newsletter article. You can use a top ten list you published in your email newsletter as a starting point for a video script.

Edit for a different audience. Also think about your different audiences and how you can put a slightly different spin on existing content to make it more relevant to a different segment of your audience.

Make short stuff longer. If you started with a two-hundred-word blog post or even a quick tweet or Facebook update, flesh that out into a newsletter article by adding some examples. Add more descriptive details, get quotes from people, or share opposing points of view.

Make long stuff shorter. Pull the headline and use it as a status update. Reduce your paragraphs to bullet points. Publish a teaser and link to the longer piece.

Change the lead. Simply start the article in a whole new way. Move something that was lower down in the article to the top. If you didn't use a quote in the first paragraph before, use one now. Open with a trend or other big-picture explanation.

Change the perspective. You can also change the perspective, so you tell the same story, but from a slightly different point of view. Maybe you're talking about three people with whom your organization has worked and you're emphasizing one of them. Tell the same basic story, but emphasize another person in the story this time.

Change the format. Start with live audio and record it as a podcast, video, or webinar recording. Have the recorded audio transcribed. Pull text from that. If you've written a how-to article, turn it into a top ten list. If you've written a top ten list about how to do something, rewrite it as an opinion piece or a review.

CREATE AN EDITORIAL CALENDAR

Step back and think about why you are communicating in the first place. Who are you trying to reach, and what are you trying to get them to do? What messages do you want to share with them, and which channels are best to carry those messages? (If you aren't sure how to answer these questions, review Part Two.)

With the answers to these big-picture questions firmly in mind, you can now create an editorial calendar to keep track of all the details. An editorial calendar is like your menu for the week, month, quarter, or year. In the calendar, you answer these basic questions:

- *Who needs to be fed?* Which audiences are you trying to reach?
- *Where do they need to be fed?* Which channels are you using to communicate? Where are you putting the content you create, and what happens to it next? Are you publishing via a newsletter, a blog, a Facebook page, or a Flickr group, for example?
- *How often do they need to be fed?* How often do you need to communicate with these people through those different channels? Are you sending out a print newsletter once a month? Are you trying to update Facebook a couple of times a week?

Editorial calendars are grids that help you see what you are going to do and when. You can use a spreadsheet or a simple table in a word processor. You can use editorial calendars to mark the deadlines when you're actually going to distribute or post content, or you can track intermediary steps too, such as when you'll conduct research, web searches, interviews, or surveys, or when you'll produce a first draft. If you have a very complicated and time-consuming approval process, mapping that out will help you meet your ultimate publishing deadlines.

An editorial calendar can also help you keep track of what's called the story arc. Although each communications piece should be able to stand on its own because it will likely be seen out of context, especially online, it's also helpful if you view each article or video as part of a larger story that you are trying to tell. Using an editorial calendar can help you map out that story arc, or how the story will progress or evolve over time. You can organize an editorial calendar in several ways.

By channel. Create a separate editorial calendar for each major communications channel that requires a significant amount of content, such as your newsletter or blog. You can also create an editorial calendar for your social networking presence as a whole.

An editorial calendar for a quarterly print newsletter could have the standing heads or placeholders for the different types of articles you typically include in your newsletter (for example, success story, donor profile), as column heads. The publication date of each issue would run as row heads in the left-hand column (see Table 10.1 for an example). You would then fill in the grid with the specific article details for each edition, such as the name of the program that the success story would come from and the name of the donor who would be profiled.

Table 10.1.
Sample Editorial Calendar for a Print Newsletter for a Local Humane Society

Article Category	Spring Edition	Summer Edition
Program Success	Spay/Neuter campaign results	How we increased our cat adoption rate
Donor or Volunteer Profile	Bill Miller—How he brokered the deal for the free dog food	Jane Smith—How she got teenagers to volunteer at the shelter
Adoption Profile	To be decided—recent dog adoption	To be decided—recent cat adoption
Pet Tips	Preparing pets for a new baby	Hot weather tips for outdoor pets
How You Can Help	Volunteer with the dog-walking program	Invite us to speak to your community group

In Every Issue: Pets Available for Adoption, In-Kind Donations Wish List, List of Donors Since Last Issue

Or let's say you want to create a weekly social media calendar to ensure that you are updating your status and contributing to the conversations on a handful of sites throughout the week. You would put each of the sites (Facebook page, Twitter profile, and so on) across the top row and the days of the week down the left-hand column. Now you can fill in as many boxes as you like with the topic you want to talk about or the kind of update you want to share (say, retweet three times, post a discussion question on the Facebook page).

By audience. You can also organize editorial calendars by audience. If you have multiple, distinct audiences (such as teachers, parents, and students) and you want to ensure that you communicate with them regularly, you might create a calendar for each audience with your channels down the side and your time frames across the top. If you have several groups of people who you're trying to reach out to and you're concerned that your communications may unconsciously favor one group or other, this method will help you find the right balance.

By program. You can also organize editorial calendars by program if you have several different programs and you want to make sure that you are spending an appropriate amount of time communicating about each one. Just as with the audience-oriented calendar, you can list your program across the top and dates down the side, then fill in the boxes with channels and specifics about the content you'll deliver there.

Once you have drafted your editorial calendars, it's helpful to add one more layer of information about priorities. Although you may plan out what you think is a reasonable calendar of blog posts for the coming month, reality can have a way of mucking up your plans. If you highlight the boxes on the grid that are "must dos" versus "would like to dos," you can more easily see how to adjust the calendar to address whatever may arise.

Behavioral scientists tell us when you put something in writing and you say exactly what you're going to do, when you're going to do it, and where you're going to do it, you're more likely to actually do it. So even if you use your editorial calendar more as a planning tool than as day-to-day guidance for your to-do list, it's still a valuable exercise to complete.

You'll find sample editorial calendars on the companion website.

WHO ARE THESE ONLINE FRIENDS, ANYWAY?

In *Trust Agents: Using the Web to Build Influence, Improve Reputation, and Earn Trust*, Chris Brogan and Julien Smith say that online friends are not the same as "move your couch" friends. An online friend is not someone you should automatically view as a fundraising prospect. Just because you are now friends on Facebook doesn't mean that your fundraising, volunteering, or advocacy appeals will be welcome. Becoming a friend online does means that the person is now open to a conversation with you. Instead of asking this new online friend to do something for you right away, learn about each other's interests and be helpful with resources. Offer several different ways to get involved that require escalating levels of commitment and let your new friends decide where they want to be on the spectrum.

ENGAGE IN CONVERSATIONS ONLINE

"Deep engagement moves our relationships with supporters from the impersonal, occasional, and transactional to the constant, loyal, and intimate," says Beth Kanter, the leading expert in how nonprofits use social media.[1] This engagement comes from ongoing conversations, whether they take place in person, online, or both. Because many of these online conversations are public, the impact of a conversation you might have with one person can be greatly multiplied as others watch or listen in. It's an entirely different way of staying in touch with your supporters and communicating about your organizations programs—one that will likely grow in importance in coming years.

Think about the conversations you have through social media as akin to a big cocktail party with lots of influential and interesting people in the room—a prime location for professional networking. To get the most out of that party, you have to work the room, but in a fairly specific way.

For example, you don't want to stand on a chair and start yelling over everyone's heads. You don't want to walk up to each person, interrupt their conversations, and thrust your business cards in their faces. People will first glare at you and then turn away completely. The same applies in social media. It's not about you. It's about, as Chris Brogan and Julien Smith say in *Trust Agents*, being "one of us." To be successful at a cocktail party and in social media, you have to see yourself and behave as a *member* of the community you are trying to reach.

You do so by sharing interesting information, being helpful to others, giving praise where it's due, and inspiring people with your stories. It doesn't hurt to have a good sense of humor too. There are always a few groups at big cocktail parties that everyone seems to gravitate to. You can usually identify them by the number of people standing around spellbound by the person in the center (or by the raucous laughter). You become the person people gravitate to online by being a helpful, friendly expert, while remaining "one of us."

Even if you are chatting with just one person at the bar and you aren't sure whether others are listening in or not, you still have to keep up your end of the conversation. Don't stare at the bottles on the wall or, worse, try to catch a glimpse of yourself in the mirror beyond while someone is talking to you. In social media, that means not only putting out your own blog posts and status updates, but responding to those posted by others. Comment on posts by leading and beginning bloggers. Link to other people's posts from your own blog. Reply and retweet on Twitter. Don't just sit and stare at your own work.

FOLLOW THE SIX GS OF MARKETING THROUGH SOCIAL MEDIA

As you consider ways to get your message out through social media, keep these six Gs of social media marketing in mind.

Good Nonprofit Marketing via Social Media Is:

Genuine. Specific people at the organization are engaging in the conversation. If we don't immediately know their names, it's easy enough to find out. They never hide behind the 501(c)(3). "Authenticity" is the current buzzword for this concept, but the idea is the same: be real.

Generous. Good marketing through social media is very much about building social capital—in other words, treating others as you wish to be treated. Promote the messages and resources of others as much as or more than your own and freely offer resources, info, help, and so forth that advance your mission. You can do so by commenting on blog posts and Facebook updates by others, retweeting on Twitter, linking to others from your own blog posts, and so on.

Grateful. You acknowledge the support and generosity of others in accomplishing your mission. You respect their contributions and share that gratitude with them and others.

Conversely, Bad Nonprofit Marketing via Social Media Is:

Greedy. Always promoting only one's organization, programs, and points of view at the exclusion of everything and everyone else.

Grandstanding. Holding up yourself or your organization as the be-all, end-all, know-it-all.

Grabby. Always trying to latch onto others or using unrelated posts or tags to get your message out. If it feels like a stretch to add some information about your organization or programs in a comment you are leaving on someone else's blog, it probably is.

CONSIDER YOUR SOCIAL MEDIA POLICY

The more your nonprofit organization engages in marketing through social media, the more likely it is that you'll need a social media policy. Look at your social media policy more as a set of guidelines and examples for staff than as hard and fast rules. Your policy should describe your overall philosophy on how your nonprofit will use social media to implement your marketing strategy and to support your mission. For some organizations, protecting the privacy of individuals that you serve will be an important element of this policy.

Representing yourself and your organization with honesty and transparency is essential to success in social media. Yet promoting that kind of openness can also raise several questions:

- What's the right mix of personal and professional information in our updates?
- What can staff talk about and what's off limits?
- What needs to be approved in advance and what can we trust to an individual's judgment?
- How and when do we respond to comments about us by others, whether positive or negative, and who responds?
- Which social media activities are deemed part of the nonprofit's marketing strategy and which are not (and therefore not encouraged during work hours)?

Your social media policy will answer these and other questions. Many nonprofits and businesses have published their social media policies online, so there is no need to start from scratch when creating yours. You'll find links to the social media policies of several nonprofit organizations on the companion website.

CONCLUSION: CONVERSATION DOES PAY OFF

If you've worked very long in nonprofit fundraising (or in venture capital, a field in which funds must also be raised), you'll recall hearing the saying, "Ask for money and you get advice. Ask for advice and you get money." Investments in nonprofits and businesses alike start with respectful conversations, often with one person asking for the advice or input of the other. Just as friendly chat at cocktail parties can lead to incredible connections that pay off big in the weeks, months, and years to come, the same is true in social media.

A July 2009 report entitled *ENGAGEMENTdb* by Charlene Li of Altimeter Group and Ben Elowitz of Wetpaint demonstrated that financial performance of the top 100 corporate brands correlates with their level of engagement in social media. Companies that are widely and deeply engaged in social media surpass other companies that are not in both revenue and profit performance. Although a similar report has yet to be produced in the nonprofit world, based on what we know so far, there is every reason to believe that a similar analysis would show that nonprofits invested in social media and actively engaging their supporters also raise more money than nonprofits who are not.

Stay in touch. Do your best to be both interesting and helpful. It works.

chapter ELEVEN

Adopt an Attitude of Gratitude

There are two kinds of gratitude: the sudden kind we feel for what we take; the larger kind we feel for what we give.

—Edwin Arlington Robinson

This chapter is about . . .

- Making gratitude central to your marketing strategy
- Improving your thank-you notes
- Publishing an annual report

All of those grandmothers across America bemoaning the demise of the written thank-you note know this truth: when you receive a well-written, personal thank-you note, you are more likely to give again and to give even more generously the next time. When you don't get a thank-you note, you remember and you probably think a little less of the recipient. Kids who want nicer gifts should wise up, and so should nonprofits.

Sending a thank-you note to a supporter is the courteous, appropriate response to a gift of any size or kind, whether it's cash, time, an introduction to an important person, or a tip about an especially helpful resource. But it's also a shrewd marketing and fundraising strategy, because it works, and because so few nonprofits do it regularly and do it well. Forget the latest-greatest fundraising success secrets and get back to basics. Adopt an attitude of gratitude and write personal, timely thank-you notes.

THE "WHAT I GOT WHEN I GAVE" EXPERIMENT

In November 2008, I cashed in forty thousand points on my Capital One credit card to make $25 donations to sixteen nonprofits. Capital One partnered with Network for Good to deliver the online donations to the charities. I specifically selected twelve national charities that I had not previously contributed to, but whose missions I support, to see what kind of communications response I would get back for my $25 gift. On the online donation form, I opted to share my contact information with the charities and provided both email and mailing addresses.

What I got when I gave was . . . almost nothing.

Of the twelve national charities I gave to, only four—a measly 33 percent—acknowledged the gift in any way. I also gave to three regional charities operating near where I live and the percentage was the same—only one of the three acknowledged the gift.

The fastest response came from National Public Radio, which sent me an email thank-you note addressed to "Dear Friend" on December 10, about two weeks after the gift. The next three responses all came within a day of each other, about six weeks after the gift was made. St. Jude's Children's Research Hospital didn't send a thank-you note, but they did add me to their monthly email newsletter list. The Alliance for Climate Protection sent a form thank-you letter, addressed to me personally. Interplast's thank-you letter was the best of the three thank-you letters, by far.

It told a story about how donations like mine are used and included before-and-after pictures of a child the program has helped by surgically correcting his cleft palette. Although my donation didn't help treat that particular child, it was very easy for me to see how my contribution could result in the very same kind of result for another child. The story in the thank-you letter reinforced that my gift would be used in the way I intended. With the exception of St. Jude's putting me on their monthly email list, I have not received follow-up correspondence from any of the organizations.

Unfortunately, the results of my giving experiment are not unusual. Others who have performed similar tests have received thank-yous from less than 50 percent of the charities.[1] These organizations will ultimately have a much more difficult time raising money, because they are forgetting one of the fundamentals of fundraising: it's easier to keep a donor you have than to find a new one. The thank-you shouldn't be seen as the end of the first gift cycle, but the beginning of the second.

As this book was going to press, I repeated the "What I Got When I Gave" experiment by once again converting credit card miles into cash donations. This time, I gave $20 each to ten national nonprofits that I had not given to previously, sharing my full contact information with the organizations. Check my blog at www.nonprofitmarketingguide.com/blog for the results.

DONORS ARE TESTING NONPROFITS, AND NONPROFITS ARE FAILING

In *Donor-Centered Research*, Penelope Burk reports that donor attrition between the first and second gift is 65 percent. In other words, 65 percent of your first-time donors don't make a second gift. That's a huge drop-off. At the same time, 75 percent of donors say their first gifts are not as generous as they could be. They are giving you only $25 even though they could afford much more, because it's the beginning of the relationship and they want to see how you're going to respond. They want to see how you will use the money and how results will be communicated back to them. They want to feel like part of the solution, not part of an ATM. Yet these statistics tell us that donors are testing nonprofits and many organizations are failing.

Burk's research shows that donors want something quite simple: a prompt, meaningful thank-you letter and additional communication that explains how the donation was used. That's it. Eighty percent of donors say that would convince them to make that second gift.

And yet the typical thank-you note that many nonprofits send out is more like a transaction receipt than a warm, personalized acknowledgment of generosity, which reinforces the ATM mentality that supporters fear. Donors are inspired to give by their hearts and their souls, and you need to give them thank-you letters that speak to their hearts and their souls, not to their checkbook.

Even if you send thank-you letters out now, odds are good that they won't stand out in your donors' minds. That's because most of these letters look and sound the same. Most thank-you letters start out the same way: "On behalf of . . ." or "Thank you for your gift of . . ." Although starting a thank-you letter that way isn't bad per se, it is predictable and tired.

Very few thank-you letters specify how the gift will be used, leaving the donor to wonder what kind of difference the gift will make if any at all. We also see thank-you notes that are just plain depressing. They emphasize how much need is still out there without making donors feel good about what they have already done with their first gift. Rather than inspiring people to give more, this approach brings people down and makes them question whether their investment in your nonprofit was a wise one.

IMPROVE YOUR THANK-YOU NOTES IN SIX STEPS

A good thank-you letter reassures donors that they have made the right decision to invest in your organization. That's how donors see themselves today—as investors in social good. This is especially true for baby boomers and younger generations, who see charitable giving as an investment of themselves in your organization. They expect to see a return on that investment. This is a significant cultural shift. The World War II generation gave out of a sense of duty and responsibility and was more trusting about how the recipient spent the money. Nowadays you need to be clear about your intentions, follow through on them, and communicate that to your supporters. This is also your opportunity to welcome new supporters into a community of others who care about your particular issue. Even if you're not a membership organization per se, you still want to create a sense of belonging to something bigger.

Let's look at several ways to improve your thank-you letters.

Get Them Out Quickly

Ideally you will send out your thank-you letters within forty-eight hours of receiving the gifts—definitely within one week. If you wait any longer than that, you risk disconnecting your letter from the gift. Keep the conversation alive by responding quickly. It can be time-consuming to write good letters, but you need to make the time, because it's not only the right thing to do but also an investment in your future financial health. I would rather see an organization spending time on creating great thank-you letters than spending time on a newsletter. Put sending your thank-you letters at the top of your communications to-do list.

Personalize Them

Use mail merge to personalize your thank-you letters so you are addressing the person by name and using specific details like the gift amount and any personal designation (such as for memorial gifts in a loved one's name). Avoid "Dear Friend" or "Dear Supporter" if at all possible. The check or credit card the donor used has a real name on it and so should the thank-you letter.

It's also a nice touch to handwrite an additional note on the letter. Nonprofits do this on fundraising solicitations all the time, and it works well on thank-you notes too. Including photos, either in the body of the letter or stuffed in an envelope, will also help personalize the letter. A photo of a client or smiling people making a difference out there in the world will light up your donor's day. Get together a group of people whom your organization helps and take a photo of them holding a big banner that says "Thank You."

You can also personalize letters by telling stories about the people you serve in the body of the letter. Even though you probably can't say right away that this $50 donation helped James, by telling James's story and how other donations have helped James, your new donor will see the connection between their gift and the types of results they can expect.

Use a More Creative Opening

Forget "On behalf of" or "Thank you for"; start your letters with a more creative and personal opening. Try something like, "You made my day" on one line by itself. Then jump into a story: "Your donation crossed my desk today and . . ." Explain how the money will be used. Or start with, "I have a great story to share with you." Launch right into a success story, then talk about how the donation will create even more happy endings. Starting with something like, "Guess what you've made possible?" is another interesting way to introduce a success story.

Jump right into these stories and save the actual thank-you verbiage for later in the letter. When you get to that point, thank the person for his or her generosity, rather than for the money. You can start with, "I am so thankful for people like you." Don't talk about the money; talk about the person. Giving money is only one way that people can make a difference.

Explain How the Gift Will Be Used

Very quickly but clearly describe a specific program for which the gift will be used. If you are fundraising for specific programs this will be easier than if you are fundraising for general support. But even then, you still need to give supporters a sense for what you're doing with the money. You can use anecdotes as examples for how the money is being spent, or you can assure donors that their gifts are going to "where the need is greatest." The more vague you are in the thank-you letter about how you are spending the gift, the more specific you should be about it when you will follow up with details about results.

Tell Them What to Expect Next

Start creating a relationship by explaining how you plan to keep the lines of communication open. Tell your donors that you will be adding them to your newsletter list and that they can unsubscribe at any time, should they choose. Most donors are going to be perfectly happy to start getting information from you. Tell them what's going to be in that newsletter, when they can expect it, and what it's going to look like so they know to look for it. Invite them to learn more about your work by visiting your website or scheduling a tour of your office. Many organizations do special briefings, lunches, or conference calls for their major donors a few times a year, so mention that you'll be inviting them to participate in those too. Also make sure they are aware of volunteer opportunities.

Personalize from the Sender, Too

Just as you are personalizing the "to" part of the letter, you also need to personalize the "from" part. Ideally, the signature is from someone with stature in the organization. Sign your letters in ink, rather than using a digital image. Even if an intern is signing your name, a real signature is better than a computer-generated one on a thank-you note. It shows that you care enough to take the time to do it.

Letters from volunteer leaders to donors can have a big impact, so if you can coordinate with your board members to get the letters out quickly, give it a try. If you can't get them all done that way, that's fine. Have the board members personalize only those thank-you letters that need to go out around the same time as the board meeting. Or ask board members to send a separate hand-written thank-you note or even an email as a follow-up to your "official" thank-you letter.

Phone calls from board members can also be really powerful, as long as you aren't asking for anything else. Simply call to say thank you and to pass on a brief success story or explanation of how the gift will be used.

Letters from clients are another great approach to personalizing the sender. If you work in any kind of human service organization with many clients who benefit from programs funded by individual donations, give this approach a try. According to Penelope Burk's research, 76 percent of donors say that getting a thank-you letter from someone who benefited from a charity's work would be very meaningful to them. Ask your clients to explain in their own words how your organization has changed their lives and to thank the donor for making it all possible.

PUBLISH AN ANNUAL REPORT

Even though nonprofit organizations aren't required to produce annual reports as publicly traded companies are, most nonprofit managers recognize the value of producing one. Annual reports can help you demonstrate your accomplishments to current and future donors, cultivate new partnerships, and recognize important people. Think of your annual report as a special kind of thank-you note.

But because annual reports aren't legally required, nonprofits often struggle with what should be included in an annual report and what should be left out. The following ten tips will help you craft an outstanding nonprofit annual report.

Focus on accomplishments, not activities. We want to know what you did, but more important, we want to know *why* you did it. What were the results? Why did you spend your time and money the way you did? What difference did it make? Connect the everyday activities of your organization to your mission statement. Don't assume that readers will automatically understand how your activities help you achieve your mission. Connect the dots for them.

Jettison the administrative minutiae. Getting a high-speed connection in the office and new accounting software may be big accomplishments from where you sit at your desk, but they have nothing to do with your mission. Inspire donors with accomplishments related to your mission in your annual report and leave all the administrative items for your board report.

Don't overemphasize fundraising accomplishments. Donors expect you to raise money, but fundraising accomplishments should not be celebrated in your annual report on the same level as your mission-related accomplishments. Readers are more interested in what you did with the money than how you raised it. Although it is appropriate to include information on how well your fundraising efforts are going, it's best to place this information in the financial section of your report, rather than front and center.

Include photos. Yes, pictures really are worth a thousand words. Many of the people reading your annual report won't actually read it. Show them what you've been doing with photos. If you don't have a digital camera, get one now. It's also fine to use stock photography to illustrate your work. Enter "royalty free stock photos" in your favorite search engine and you'll find numerous sites.

Write captions that tell your story. Now that you've got them looking at the photos, tell a story with your captions. Don't just state what's in the photo. Connect the photo to an accomplishment. If people read nothing but the captions in your annual report, they should still get a sense for the good work you did last year.

Include personal profiles. Donors will be more impressed with real stories about real people than general summaries of your work. Explain what you have accomplished overall, then humanize your statistics with some personal profiles. Highlight how your work helped a specific individual. Share a volunteer's story of how they made a positive difference.

Explain your financials. Many of your donors won't know how to read a financial statement or won't take the time to read it. Include a paragraph or two that explains in plain English what the tables say. Where does your money come from and how do you spend it? What are your main fundraising strategies? Did you implement any cost-savings measures this year?

If you need space, trim the donor lists. Nonprofits need to strike a balance between using the space in their annual reports to discuss their accomplishments and using it to recognize donors. If as much as half of your annual report is donor lists, you should consider scaling the lists back to make more room for text and photos. Smaller donors can be recognized in other ways, such as lists in newsletters.

Triple-check your donor lists. There's no better way to sabotage a future donation than to spell the donor's name wrong in your annual report. If you are uncertain about a name, don't guess. Check it with the donor. Also carefully check the names of government agencies and foundations that gave you grants. The names people call these organizations in conversation are often shorthand for the full legal names that belong in your annual report.

Tell donors how they can help. Never leave potential supporters hanging, wondering how they can help you. Once you've inspired them with the good works in your annual report, close by telling them how they can help you do more. How can they support you with their money or time? Do you offer planned giving options, for example? Will you accept gifts of stock? Can they use a credit card? Be clear about the best ways to help.

These tips work best if you are producing a traditional annual report of at least eight pages. But alternate formats can work too, including two- or four-pagers, slideshows, and videos. See the companion website for tips on creating these kinds of annual reports.

ON THE WEB

CONCLUSION: STOP MAKING EXCUSES; MAKE THE TIME INSTEAD

When I talk to nonprofits about how important it is to write thank-you notes, I often feel like a nag. Perhaps even you felt nagged reading this chapter! But the reason I'm devoting an entire chapter of this book to them is because responding to the generosity of your supporters with gratitude really is a core element of a successful nonprofit marketing program.

Don't say you don't have the time for something this important. Give higher priority to your thank-you notes than to any other piece of communication you work on. The newsletter doesn't go out, the website doesn't get updated, and your report to your board doesn't get done until you have sent your thank-you letters to your donors. Failing to do so is a sure road to remaining underfunded and understaffed. Following through is the path to even more generosity from your supporters.

chapter
TWELVE

Empower Your Fans to Build More Support for You

It is amazing what you can accomplish if you do not care who gets the credit.

—Harry S. Truman

This chapter is about . . .

- Identifying your organization's biggest fans
- Building social capital
- Empowering your fans to market your cause by friendraising and fundraising

You are doing a great job keeping in touch and making your supporters feel welcomed into a network of people who care about your organization and your good cause by communicating with them regularly and frequently. You are offering your supporters the kind of information they want, when they want it, thanking them for their support, and optimizing opportunities for two-way conversations. You are keeping it all organized with a content creation strategy and editorial calendar. Now what?

As you get to know your supporters, you'll find that some percentage of them—perhaps 5 percent or maybe as much as 20 percent—are not just average supporters, but truly big fans who want do whatever they can to help you. In this chapter, we'll look what makes someone a fan, how to make them feel even better about your organization, and ways to encourage them to build even more support for your cause.

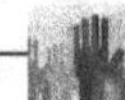

UNFAMILIAR WITH SOME OF THE TERMS IN THIS CHAPTER?

If you find some of the terminology in this section foreign or confusing, refer to the Glossary of Online Marketing Terms at the back of the book.

IDENTIFY YOUR WALLFLOWERS, BUDDIES, AND FANS

The people who make up your various lists of supporters (mailing lists, blog subscribers, social networking friends, and so on) usually fall into one of three categories: wallflowers, buddies, or fans.

Wallflowers. They are in touch with you, but prefer to keep to themselves. They subscribe to your newsletter or blog and wish you well, but they don't actively participate by volunteering, donating, or advocating for your cause. In online parlance, they are lurkers, which sounds negative, but isn't. It just means they are the quiet ones who pay attention to what's going on but don't actively participate. The conventional wisdom of "participation inequality"[1] is that lurkers make up 90 percent of online communities. When you see that your email newsletter is being opened by only 15 percent of the people receiving it,[2] you may wonder who the other 85 percent are. They are your wallflowers: they want to stay on your list, but they only occasionally read what you send them.

Buddies. Buddies like your organization and what you do. They sometimes volunteer time, donate money, or attend your events. They'll sometimes comment on your blog posts and occasionally forward your newsletter to their friends. But if you don't ask them to act, they probably won't do it on their own. Buddies, or intermittent contributors, make up 9 percent of online communities. They represent part of the 15 percent of nonprofit e-newsletters that do get opened. When you ask people on your email list to take an action, they'll do so one to five times per year, and as a group will represent two-thirds of all actions taken.

Fans. Fans regularly connect with you and your cause and spread the word to others without being asked to do so, because they love what you do and being associated with your good cause. Although they are relatively few compared to the size of your buddy and wallflower groups, they are your most loyal volunteers, donors, and advocates and are therefore incredibly powerful. Fans, or heavy contributors, make up just 1 percent of online communities. They will nearly always be a part of the group that's responsible for the 2 percent click-through rate for nonprofit e-newsletters. They are also the 7 percent of people on your email list who take six or more of your requested actions, representing 31 percent of the total actions taken. You'll sometimes see your fans called patrons, evangelists, or über-friends.

You can *convert wallflowers into buddies* by continuing to share positive news, offering helpful resources, and building up trust in your organization over time. Make it easy to get involved by offering a variety of options that don't require a long-term commitment. Then when you happen to mention a program or opportunity that matches their values perfectly, many of them will step up.

You can *convert buddies into fans* by thanking them personally for what they do and reporting back on the difference they are making. Always reinforce that when they do take some kind of action, it really does make a difference. Think about ways to reward your buddies, by offering them some kind of special status or publicly acknowledging them at in-person events and through your social networking connections (such as retweeting or replying on Twitter or "liking" or commenting on Facebook).

However, for a small but very important group, this is only the beginning. For your most interested and active supporters—your biggest fans—you need to do more than stay in touch. You need to fully engage them in your work and reward them for their support by making them feel like part of the team. It takes a personal, conversational, one-on-one touch that can happen offline, online, or both.

You want to turn casual supporters into true friends—friends who advocate for your cause and organization within their own networks and beyond, who support you financially, and who help you in ways you never imagined. You want to create bonds between these friends and build a strong and extensive social network of people who are there for you. But it's a two-way street, and that means you need to be there for them too.

WHAT MAKES SOMEONE A FAN?

The qualities of the biggest fans of your organization are not all that different from what makes someone a big fan of a sports team.

There's an emotional connection. Your cause touches something deep inside of your supporters and makes them willing to do crazy things for you. Sports fans paint their faces and wear crazy costumes. Your fans might do something many would consider equally crazy, like hosting a party in their own home, inviting all of their friends over, paying for the food, and then giving you the floor to talk about your cause while they ask their friends to empty their wallets. To top it off, they'll write a big check themselves, one of many over the course of their relationship with your organization. Or they might do the online equivalent, such as placing one of your fundraising widgets on their own blogs and emailing all of their friends about you. They might call in a big favor, but on your behalf instead of their own.

They believe they matter. Your biggest fans believe their actions will have a real impact—and you can't do it without them. Fans bring signs and cheer and chant, because they believe it will inspire their teams to play better. Your biggest fans also believe that their support really matters and that they are making it possible for you to do your best and to bring about real changes to make the world a better place.

They want to belong. Your biggest fans want to feel like they are part of something bigger than themselves. Sports fans dress in the team colors and do the wave. Your biggest fans also want to feel like they are part of something bigger by seeing how their individual contributions, combined with others, can produce something amazing. Many of the challenges in the world today seem impossible to address as an individual. But when individuals become part of your team, they can see how their small contribution adds up to so much more. Make them feel like they really are valued members of your team.

It feels good. Your biggest fans also get a "helper's high"—a feeling of well-being and happiness that's been scientifically documented in volunteers. Sports fans party in the stands, hanging out with friends and having a good time. Your fans get a boost too, because giving feels good, both emotionally and physically.

GIVE YOUR BIGGEST FANS THE PERSONAL TOUCH

A supporter's interest in helping your organization always starts with their values, not yours. People support nonprofits who reinforce their own value systems.

That means you need to pay attention to what they specifically care about and start there as you develop a relationship with your supporters.

If you operate multiple programs, for example, it's likely that your biggest fans care much more about the success of one of those programs than all the others, because that one program touches them in some very personal way. Don't assume that a supporter who is investing many hours a week to make your "puppy manners class" for new dog owners a success will be equally enthused about fundraising to build a new playroom for cats awaiting adoption.

I made an unsolicited donation to a children's health charity after watching a news program about the incredible work they were doing in the Gulf Coast helping children whose lives had been turned upside down by Hurricanes Katrina and Rita. My donation was designated on their website donation form specifically for this program in the Gulf Coast. I might very well have become a life-long supporter of the group, except the next solicitation they sent me was about reducing childhood asthma in New York City. They disconnected me from my original reason for giving, and I disconnected from them as a donor.

Your biggest fans deserve special, personal treatment. Even a small organization can provide personal treatment to some percentage of its biggest fans. Even if you can't get to everyone, start with some of them. Ask board members or other volunteer leaders to help by playing the role of "ambassador" to your biggest fans. Ask each person to personally call a short list of key supporters a few times a year, to send handwritten thank-you notes, to write personal notes on the top of their newsletters, or to forward an email about something in the news that they believe the fan will find particularly interesting.

When you treat your cause's fans like true friends, amazing things can happen. Consider the experience that John Bell, the development director for the Conservation Trust for North Carolina (CTNC), recently had with one of the group's major donors, an older woman we'll call Ann Smith.

Ann's ancestors came from a particular county in the North Carolina mountains that John knows well, and he and Ann share a love of history and vernacular architecture. John realized that another nonprofit group he belonged to was hosting a fundraiser at a pioneer home that was once in Ann's family. Ann had not seen the home in many years and was thrilled when John invited her to attend the fundraiser with him, including driving her there.

Ann also serves on a local college's library board. When John was traveling through the area where Ann's ancestors had come from, he noticed a history book about that county in a local bookstore. John bought the book and sent it to the college library for their collection. The library placed a nameplate in the book that reads "Given in honor of Ann Smith" and sent a card to Ann acknowledging John's gift.

When John saw an article in the *New York Times* that reminded him of an issue that Ann had once worked on in another state, he cut out the article and sent it to her.

In one of their recent conversations, Ann informed John of a large six-figure bequest to CTNC.

John didn't bring Ann to the event, buy the book in her honor, and send her the newspaper clipping with any expectation that she would include his organization in her estate plans. He did all these things because he values Ann not only as a CTNC supporter but also as a friend with interests far beyond the cause he represents. He's invested time in that friendship, getting to know Ann as a person. If he hadn't really paid attention to who Ann is and listened to her, he wouldn't have been able to make any of these heartfelt personal gestures that helped build this friendship.

Before joining CTNC, John raised funds for a civil rights foundation, an AIDS services organization, a health clinic, a homeless shelter, and low-income housing, and he has many similar stories to share, as do most successful development directors. "It's morally repugnant and cynical—and ultimately futile—to try to make donors give just by being kind, or generous, or considerate," says John. "Like in all relationships, practice the Golden Rule. A donor relationship will grow stronger if you think more about the other person than about yourself."

BUILD UP YOUR SOCIAL CAPITAL

The formal name for what you are building by giving your fans the personal touch is "social capital." Time, money, and skills are clearly valuable. But so is whom you know and how willing they are to help you. Social capital is the willingness of people to help each other, and it can be viewed just like any other resource your nonprofit marketing program needs in order to succeed. This is especially true if you don't have enough time or money to run your marketing program the way you'd like.

Banking social capital is much easier than it sounds: be nice, be helpful, and most important, don't expect anything in return from those you are nice and helpful to. Do as much as you can for as wide a network as you can. Eventually, and most likely through circuitous routes you could never predict, you will be on the receiving end of equal amounts of kindness and aid—perhaps even more. Pay it forward, and it will make its way back around to you.

I spoke on a nonprofit marketing panel with David Zermeno, executive director of Operation P.E.A.C.E., a Neighborhood Network center in Boston. David shared several great stories about how simply being nice to people and providing really good customer service had created wonderful opportunities for his organization—perhaps more so than any other traditional marketing tactics. Here's one of David's stories in his own words:[3]

> One day Gloria, a senior citizen, came into my center saying, "What's this email thing all about? My daughter-in-law keeps asking me to take a computer class and get an email account so we can communicate throughout the day. She won't get off my back, but I hate computers. I'm so afraid of them. Do you think you can help me?"
>
> The first thing I did was make sure she felt welcome the minute she walked in the door. "Thank you so much for coming in, Gloria," I said. "Don't be afraid," said the other seniors in my computer class for seniors. "We all had the same fear when we started." "You see that?" I said. "I've never met anyone who I couldn't help. So have a seat; I'll have you up and running with email in no time." As I starting teaching her, I just tapped her on the shoulder and focused on her quick progress.
>
> With her new email account, she became a regular in my computer class for senior citizens every Monday morning where they listen to jazz music and use my class as a community of hip seniors who have access to technology.
>
> Shortly afterwards, Gloria told me her daughter-in-law was very happy and impressed with my computer program for senior citizens. Having an ability to communicate as a family throughout the day, their emails had brought them closer together and had clearly strengthened their relationship.
>
> One day her daughter-in-law called to personally thank and inform me of a grant that was intended to serve community programs like

my program for seniors. She strongly encouraged me to apply and gave me a lot of important information. She also informed me that she was also on the panel and would make sure that the trustees knew what a difference my programs were making for families like hers. I couldn't have a better person as an advocate for my proposal. It was valuable marketing that money could not buy.

Social capital is all about trading in trust, authority, access, and influence. John and Ann; David, Gloria, and Gloria's daughter-in-law; all of them shared these qualities with each other. It is all rooted in basic human kindness. It's impossible to say who your next Ann or Gloria will be, and if you are trying to pick them out of the crowd, you are missing the point.

HELP FANS SEE THEIR STORY IN YOUR STORY

My friend and fundraising expert Gail Perry tells nonprofit development staff to take their boards and donors on site tours and to introduce them to the people they serve, then ask "What are your impressions?" This is a great way to get your supporters to open up about why they care so much about your cause and, even more important, to make "your" story into "their" story and to more fully engage your biggest fans in your work. Rather than simply telling your supporters a story, you are giving them the opportunity to create one themselves out of their own experiences and then to share it with others.

As you talk about the success of your organization, include your biggest fans in those stories. Make them the heroes and heroines. Give them the credit. If our animal rescue group saved twenty-five cats last month, we could publish a straightforward article that focused on those statistics and how they came about. But it would be much more powerful and inclusive to talk about the story of just one of those cats and the person who made her rescue possible—one of your biggest fans. Tell the story of the volunteer who found the kitten in the drain pipe, injured and starving. Show a picture of the kitten sleeping on the pink fuzzy pillows of the little girl whose family adopted her—another big fan. We could end the story by saying something like, "We had twenty-five happy endings just like this one in March."

BE CLEAR ABOUT THE BEST WAYS FOR PEOPLE TO HELP

Some of your fans will prefer to give money, others will prefer to give time. Some of your fans will be outgoing and love meeting new people in person; others will prefer to network online. The fastest way to lose a fan is to insist that there is only one way to offer support—your way. You'll burn out your supporters if you ask them to do things they don't really want to do. Instead, create a flexible, diverse list of ways that your fans can help you, and let each person decide what's best for her. Just as every member of your staff is a marketer (like it or not), think of all of your fans as special envoys of your marketing team to the rest of the world.

"How can someone who loves this organization help you?" When I ask a nonprofit this question, I'm always a little surprised to get a blank stare in return. Or worse: answers that involve stuffing envelopes, filing paperwork, and other mundane tasks. If someone says, "How can I help you?" always be ready with at least three options. These should change given what's going on in your office, the time of year, and what's needed most. Once a month, sit down with your staff and come up with your wish list for volunteer help. Then make sure your fans know what's on that list so they can help you find the right people. Use a question from a supporter, like "How can I help?" to start a conversation. Reply with a question of your own: what do you enjoy doing or what are you interested in learning more about?

Even if all of your programmatic needs are met, every nonprofit can suggest two opportunities that help market your cause: friendraising and microfundraising.

ENCOURAGE YOUR FANS TO FRIENDRAISE

Even if you don't need volunteers in the traditional sense, there's always something that people who care about your cause can do for you, and it's called friendraising. Fundraising is scary to many people, but friendraising is easier. Simply ask your big fan to tell five of their friends about you in whatever way is most comfortable for them. They can talk about your nonprofit over lunch or coffee or on Facebook.

Research and practical experience shows that we are most effectively persuaded to do something when our friends, family, and colleagues are the ones doing the talking. Consider this take on the 2008 presidential election by Colin Delany of epolitics.com: "Elections are won at the water cooler, at the bar, at the dinner table, over the phone, and in bed, and Obama's supporters were primed to know the message, know the strategy, and understand the stakes every time his candidacy came up in conversation . . . [The campaign succeeded] because of one basic idea: that you can trust people to work on your behalf if you give them the tools and the training." Can you say the same about your supporters? If not, why not?

The beauty of online marketing and Web 2.0 is that it is so easy for friends to pass info on to other friends. You can build your network of friends of friends of supporters of your organization incredibly fast online. Here are some of the tools you can offer fans to help with friendraising:

- Create content about your issues that fans can freely use in their own blogs, social networking profiles, newsletters, and so on. Think about how-to articles, success stories, top ten lists, question-and-answer interviews, and other favorite formats.
- Find a way to solve a problem that people care about. Share it with your fans so they can share it with others.
- Give fans the missing resources or tools they need to make a difference on their own. What's missing? Ask your fans! They'll tell you.
- Give them step-by-step help on how to donate online, upload videos, and the like. Even if they don't need this help themselves, people in their networks probably will. Help your fans be helpful to their own friends.

ENCOURAGE YOUR FANS TO MICROFUNDRAISE

The thought of asking someone for hundreds or thousands of dollars scares many people. On the other hand, asking for $5 or $10, especially for a good cause, is much more doable. The nonprofit jargon for this concept is "microphilanthropy" or "peer-to-peer fundraising" and it's been going on for decades as friends "sponsor" friends in events like 5K walks. The concept is now being used online via social media.

One of your fans decides to ask her network of friends to make a small donation to your organization (almost always under $50 and typically much less). Some of her friends also send on the request to their own networks, creating a viral effect.

One of the first and biggest trials of this concept happened between December 13, 2007, and January 31, 2008, when the Case Foundation challenged American nonprofits to see how many donors they could find to contribute online to their cause in two events, America's Giving Challenge with *Parade* magazine and the Causes Giving Challenge on Facebook. Participating nonprofits were judged not on the amount of money they raised but on the number of donors they recruited. Five people donating $10 each was more much valuable than one person donating $50.

As reported by Beth Kanter and Allison H. Fine in *America's Giving Challenge: Assessment and Reflection Report* for the Case Foundation, the most successful causes in the contest were those with champions who reached out to their own friends, family, colleagues, and coworkers first. They connected first with people they knew personally, whether those contacts were familiar with the cause or not.

Because the personal connections are so powerful, smaller organizations, including those run exclusively by volunteers, were successful in the contest. Eleven of the sixteen winning charities had annual organization budgets of less than $1 million and most of the champions were not professional fundraisers. According to the report, cause champions who were inexperienced fundraisers reported that asking people they knew to give $10 was easy, but sending impersonal group emails was completely ineffective. One volunteer is quoted as saying, "I realized that 90 percent of the people who gave were personally asked by me or one of our volunteers. Email blasts and canned messaging does not work. What works is short quick messages asking for the $10."

This is consistent with research from the private sector as well. A 2008 online survey by North American Technographics found that consumers trust an email from people they know far more than any other source of online information. Seventy-seven percent of survey respondents trusted a personal email, whereas only 28 percent trusted an email from a company or brand (akin to your organization's own email newsletter).

You can use two tactics that worked for the Case Foundation—deadlines and competitions—when you ask your fans to fundraise for you.

You'll do better with requests that are both timely and urgent. Unfortunately, many nonprofits tie this motivation to a negative: "If you don't give by this date, this bad thing will happen." Instead, tie the deadline to something positive, like winning a contest or raising funds through a matching grant.

Nonprofits have been using competition as a motivation for many years because it works. Teams of office workers compete in races. Board members compete to see how many new members they can recruit. A friendly competition with clear and fair rules can be a great motivator, especially when participants can track their progress against others. America's Giving Challenge used an online leaderboard updated in real time. Participants in that competition said the leaderboard was instrumental in encouraging them to do well.

The second America's Giving Challenge took place at the end of 2009. Check the companion website for lessons learned from this round.

APPROACH NEW FRIENDS OF FRIENDS

Your biggest fans spread the word for you and even collect money for you. Now how do you bring those new people they've introduced to your cause into your community and transform them from wallflowers to buddies to fans? The standard advice is to come up with a cultivation campaign that introduces these new people to the organization over time and encourages them to become directly involved with the nonprofit as a volunteer or donor, as if they had discovered the organization on their own.

The problem is that this treats the person we'll call the Original Fan like some kind of inconvenient or spent middleman. For many nonprofits, the Original Fan is anything but a middleman; instead, he or she is more like a gatekeeper or nightclub bouncer. It's only through the Original Fan that the nonprofit will have access to those people and their wallets.

Most national organizations with widely understood or broadly supported missions should probably go ahead and try to establish direct relationships with all of those friends of friends. But nonprofits with specific geographic limitations or niche missions (for example, diseases that affect relatively few people) should move forward much more carefully and deliberately, checking to see just how likely it is that the friends of friends will actually convert into long-term, direct donors. Many of these friends of friends will be just one-time givers, and that's OK.

For example, I donated money to a food bank in New Jersey because my friend Nancy asked me to as part of her Facebook Causes birthday celebration. Although I certainly support the mission of food banks in general, I live in North Carolina. Nancy is the sole reason that I donated to this food bank in New Jersey. No matter how many newsletters or appeal letters the New Jersey food bank might send me in the future, it is extremely unlikely that I will ever give them another dime.

Unless, of course, Nancy—the Original Fan—asks me to.

That's why when the executive director of a local HIV/AIDS group for whom I fundraised as part of my Facebook Causes birthday celebration asked me whether she should add the names of my donating friends to her prospect database, I told her no. I serve on the board of directors of this particular organization, so that's why I was asked. (I doubt that few Original Fans are consulted in this way at all—which is part of the problem.) Instead, I asked her to send a thank-you note directly to my donating friends and invite them to sign up for the e-newsletter if they wanted to. I've asked her not to message these people again otherwise. As the Original Fan, I know these people are giving because of me, because I asked—not really because of the cause. Although I'm sure that everyone who donated supports the mission of the chosen organization, just as I support food banks, nearly all of the people who donated lived outside the geographic service area, and I believe it's extremely unlikely that they would give again on their own.

Unless, of course, I—the Original Fan—asked them to.

Although you should definitely spend some time coming up with cultivation strategies for friends of friends, it is equally important—and I'd argue *more* important for local or niche organizations—to develop strategies to keep your Original Fans fully engaged and willing to fundraise for you again and again.

The food bank and HIV/AIDS group don't need strategies to reach Nancy's friends and my friends; they need strategies to keep Nancy and me and all their other Original Fans happy with the organization and excited about its work so that we will continue to tap our networks on their behalf.

EMPOWER YOUR BIGGEST FANS: LESSONS FROM THE OBAMA CAMPAIGN

Colin Delany of epolitics.com has published a wonderful, free e-book called *Learning from Obama: Lesson for Online Communicators in 2009 and Beyond.* I recommend that you read the guide cover to cover, but here's the main lesson: treat your supporters as a resource to be maintained with great care. Whether you voted for Obama or not, you cannot argue with the online acumen of his campaign and the record-breaking fundraising prowess that was propelled in large part by small donors who gave again and again and again. Here are some additional lessons from the campaign.

Make it easy to find, forward, and act. By creating a simple, focused website, the campaign used the site as a supporter-grabbing machine, encouraging visitors to sign up from their first click. The site was easy to navigate and provided links to tools on every page, never missing a chance to turn a visitor into a convert.

Channel online enthusiasm into specific, targeted activities that further your goals. The campaign maintained a presence on fifteen different social networking sites and leveraged all of those platforms by directing people back to the MyBarackObama website, where they could then channel supporters into specific activities. They offered tiers of engagement to get as much out of supporters as they were willing to give.

Trust your supporters to help you. To keep volunteers motivated and working, the campaign let them in on strategy details that most campaigns closely guard. They closed the loop by letting them see how their efforts fit into a larger framework, including online video briefings. Providing both in-person and video training was also important to this strategy. Because they based their outreach on volunteer commitment rather than strict message control, the campaign not only embraced but celebrated the potential in all of these supporters talking to their own networks of friends and family, in their own words.

Empower them to take action themselves and to represent you when you can't do it yourself. MyBarackObama.com gave supporters everything they needed to run their own events, fundraising campaigns, and even speak to the press, and the site was particularly important in areas where the campaign didn't have professional staff. They also encouraged supporters to create their own Facebook groups based on a specific location or interest, even though the campaign ran its own Facebook page and group, because they realized that all of these separate groups expanded rather than diluted Obama's outreach to supporters.

Focus on incremental improvements. The campaign didn't aim for immediate perfection in its communications, but instead incrementally improved both their tools and messages through testing and experience. The campaign was constantly testing its emails, measuring differences produced by various senders' names, subject lines, topics, text, imagery, and link placement.

Build your lists through the integration of offline and online tactics. The campaign included www.BarackObama.com on everything used offline, from backdrops at speeches to yard signs. They collected email addresses and cell phone numbers at rallies.

CONCLUSION: GIVE AND YOU SHALL RECEIVE

Like many organizations, the 1010 Project, which works on global poverty issues from its office in Denver, made its first foray into social media by setting up a Facebook group, a MySpace page, and a small presence on YouTube—and then forgot about them. Tim Brauhn, the fundraising coordinator, described the group's website as "horrifying, hard to navigate, and most of all, boring." The 1010 Project had successfully used word-of-mouth marketing offline as a key strategy to bring new people to the group, yet they were failing to do the same thing online. "We had no real interaction online with our fans and supporters," says Tim.

Their first step to correct this problem was to redesign their website to allow for more storytelling, including the addition of a blog. They also jumped headfirst into Twitter, concentrating on finding both individuals and other nonprofits interested in their international development niche. "The 1010 Project spends time on Twitter talking about world poverty, but we also use our reach to promote other nonprofits, especially in Colorado but also worldwide," says Tim. "The sharing is reciprocated." They also went back to Facebook and YouTube and added more content there.

Now the 1010 Project has a robust social media presence—and it's paying off. "Twitter followers regularly lump us in with huge organizations like Save the Children or Oxfam," says Tim. "With an advertising/marketing budget of approximately $0 and lots of interns, we've grown our web traffic by 300 percent in the last year and drastically increased the depth of our interaction with all sorts of audiences. We've got lots of cheerleaders out there, and maybe a thousand new contacts," says Tim. "We made a decision to jump into the Net and to lose control of the brand a little bit. It has paid us back in spades."

You can't market your organization on your own. Expand your marketing team by giving your biggest fans something to cheer about, helping them spread their enthusiasm to others, and rewarding them with your time and attention. Give and you shall receive.

PART FOUR

Doing It Yourself Without Doing Yourself In

Every project or program, no matter how big or small, depends on a mixture of three ingredients: time, talent, and treasure. How much time can you devote to marketing, and how can you get others to offer their time? What can you do yourself, what other talent do you have on staff, and what tasks do you need to hire out? How much money do you have available and how should you spend it? We'll look at each of these three elements in this part. Chapter Thirteen explores ways to get more done in less time. Chapter Fourteen provides tips on building your pool of talent, both from within yourself and by working with others. Chapter Fifteen reveals ways to market your good cause on a tight budget.

chapter
THIRTEEN

Find the Time: Get More Done in Fewer Hours

The great difference between those who succeed and those who fail does not consist in the amount of work done by each, but in the amount of intelligent work.

—Og Mandino

This chapter is about . . .

- Saving time by learning from others
- Getting fear out of the way
- Getting organized and using time-saving tools

You will never have enough time to do everything you want to do to market your organization and your good cause, especially if you are doing it on your own. Like any other busy professional, you need to learn some basic work-life management skills so that your email box and to-do list don't run or ruin your life (David Allen's Getting Things Done (GTD) model is a popular one now). But that's not what this chapter is about. Instead, the strategies in this chapter will help you work not only faster but smarter, both strategically and tactically, on your nonprofit marketing program.

KEEP UP WITH BEST PRACTICES, BIG BRAINS, AND COOL KIDS

I'm not fond of the term "best practices" because it implies that some great genius out there has blessed a certain way of doing things, and the rest of us don't need to bother with innovating or seeing what really works for us. But I do like what the concept stands for: that we should learn from what has worked for others, and that by doing so we'll get a head start down the right path. That's much better, especially when pressed for time, than scratching around for where to begin and fumbling around on our own. With this definition in mind, this book is full of best practices. But best practices do and should change as people collaborate and share results. Often you need to settle for something that your gut tells you will work, or something that's seems good enough, rather than waiting around for the best solution possible.

With all that said, you will save a tremendous amount of time if you keep track of what others are doing and watch for successful patterns. In the nonprofit marketing world, your colleagues around the country are quite generous with sharing specific case studies at conferences and online. We are lucky to have a talented pool of bloggers both wide and deep who share great real-world advice. Nonprofit communicators, especially those who are interested in social media and online fundraising, are well represented on Twitter. If you are given a new task that you don't know how to perform, a search of the nonprofit blogosphere or a question on Twitter will nearly always point you in the right direction.

Best practices will get you started on the right path, but to see what's around the bend, you need to pay attention to a different set of people—"big brains" and "cool kids." Big brains are the smart people not only in nonprofit marketing but also in related fields like technology, social media, and small business marketing. They have moved beyond today's conventional wisdom and are looking at how the world is changing right now so they can think through what we should all be doing tomorrow. Katya Andresen and Beth Kanter are two perpetual big brains in our field. Cool kids are nonprofit organizations, usually with ample resources to experiment, who are not shy about sharing their experiences. The Humane Society of the United States and the National Wildlife Federation are two of the cool kids in nonprofit marketing through social media.

For my list of recommended big brains and cool kids to watch, visit the companion website. It's like an ounce of prevention for your marketing program.

You'll save a tremendous amount of effort and time if you simply schedule a few minutes each day to read up on what others are talking about.

GET FEAR OUT OF THE WAY

After trying to reinvent the proverbial wheel, the next biggest time waster in the nonprofit marketing world is fear—your own fear and the fear of decision makers around you. It's frustrating to develop a new creative project or campaign only to be shut down because the decision makers just don't understand it or are too afraid to give it a shot. Many nonprofit marketing decisions, especially about content, are made out of fear. Will people be upset if we say that? Is this design too "out there" for us? Many nonprofits fall into the trap of overly conservative marketing because of fear. Try to delve into exactly what those fears are so you can address them.

To help decision makers feel more comfortable with what you are proposing, try one or more of the following methods:

- Clear up misconceptions about your target audience, which are often at the root of marketing fears, by really getting to know them (review Chapters Three and Four for tips).
- Share case studies from other organizations that demonstrate how what you are suggesting can be successful.
- Do a small test run of your idea first to see how it works out. Adjust accordingly.
- Hold an informal focus group on your idea, so that decision makers feel like their input has been heard.
- Develop review and approval procedures to ensure that you include in the process all the people who really do need to be included.
- Create a crisis plan to deal with the worst-case scenario, should it actually happen.

At the 2009 National Technology Conference, Clay Shirky, author of *Here Comes Everybody: The Power of Organizing Without Organizations*, told nonprofits to "Fail informatively. Fail like crazy." Here's what he meant: You should try lots of different things at once (but not *too* many), especially with online marketing and social media, because both the expense and the risk of colossal failure are so small, and the potential benefits are so huge. You have so much to learn through experimenting. Then share what you learn with others, and learn from what they share with you.

Hand wringing consumes far too much time that should be spent with fingers tapping on the keyboard. Try something new, without fear. Let everyone know what you are doing, keep track of what happens, and report the results. People will be so pleasantly surprised by your refreshing transparency that they'll forget to be upset with you about the experiments that don't quite go off as you hoped.

UNFAMILIAR WITH SOME OF THE TERMS IN THIS CHAPTER?

If you find some of the terminology in this section foreign or confusing, refer to the Glossary of Online Marketing Terms at the back of the book.

AVOID THE SOCIAL MEDIA TIME SINK

Many nonprofits are afraid to try marketing their organizations through social media simply because they fear it will take too much time. But if you are focused on why you are using the tools (that is, you know who you are connecting with and why, or you have a specific goal, like researching trends on a particular subject area), then social media can be quite manageable. It should go without saying that employees should limit the amount of time they spend at work on personal tasks—whether that's on the phone, over email, or within social media—yet that seems to be a big concern for nonprofit leaders. Be clear about your expectations and trust your staff to follow through.

Personal time aside, working in social media does require regular attention. It's all about having conversations with other people, so you do need to check in regularly and stick with it to reap any benefits from those relationships. However, there are several easy ways to ensure that you don't spend more time than you want to.

Use an RSS reader. Don't waste time visiting a bunch of different blogs. Have them send their fresh content to you, so you can quickly scan posts and decide which ones you want to comment on. Learn more about setting up your RSS reader in Chapter Three.

Set limits. Using any one of several free tools, you can clock the amount of time you spend on various websites. Decide how much time you should spend on each of the social media sites, or how much you want to spend on social media as a whole, then budget that time accordingly. When you reach your limit for the day, log out of your profile and don't log back in until the next day.

You can also limit yourself to certain parts of the day. If you take a lunch break at noon and you want to spend only fifteen minutes a day on social media, log in at 11:45. If you go over, you miss your lunch break. Same goes for doing it at the end of the day. Do you really want to work late? It's up to you.

Automate your updates. Several tools can speed up your pace and save time in social media. For example, you can update your status on Twitter, Facebook, and other sites at one time. Use these tools cautiously, however, to avoid too much duplication. Other tools will let you schedule tweets or blog posts to appear at later times, so you can do all of your original postings at once, limiting the time you spend daily to replies and commenting on others' posts. You'll find specific recommendations for which tools to use on the companion website.

ON THE WEB

Streamline by using complementary tools. Twitter and Facebook work together for quick conversations. Move longer conversations to a blog, email, or a phone call.

Make sure quality trumps quantity. This applies to the number of followers you have, as well as how often you update or post. Focus on what will have the most impact in the limited amount of time you are allowing.

Use filters to see what matters most. All social media sites have either built-in tools or additional applications that help you see what's most important to you. Use lists in Facebook to group your Facebook friends together. Use Twitter lists or groups in Twitter applications like Seesmic or TweetDeck to group people you follow. That way if you don't have much time, you can check in with the people who are the most important to you at any given time.

Set realistic goals for your social media presence. Nina Simon, author of the Museum 2.0 blog, has some great suggestions for how to approach social media marketing, based on how much time you have to spend on it per week. *Have one to five hours per week? Be a participant.* Reply to what others are saying on their own blogs, review sites, and Flickr and YouTube. You can also set up a very basic Twitter feed or Facebook page and update it once or twice a week. *Have five to ten hours per week? Be a content provider.* Start a blog or a podcast. *Have ten to twenty hours per week?* Be a community director. Build your own online community that allows your supporters to upload their own content and mix it in with yours. Let supporters contribute directly to your databases with tagging systems. Explore virtual communities like Second Life.

It's possible to participate in social media without actually creating the content yourself. Instead, comment on what others are producing. That's the strategy adopted by TransForm, an advocate for public transportation and walkable communities in the San Francisco Bay Area. "We were feeling a bit overwhelmed by social media. We knew we needed to get in on the action, but were so limited in terms of time," explains Marta Lindsey, TransForm's communications and development director.

Instead of blogging themselves, they decided to diligently follow the top blog on their issues, sf.streetsblog.org. "By really listening to what the community there talked about and seeing what stories this blog was interested in, we were able to join in a lot of conversations that were relevant to our issues and build up a great relationship with the blog so that we can go to them with stories and get coverage there," says Marta.

Without having to maintain its own blog and build a following of subscribers, TransForm is still part of the conversation, where the people most interested in its issues already are. "I feel like we have established ourselves now as a key nonprofit working on these issues—and as an expert and strong advocate. We've seen a notable increase in web traffic, especially after we've had stories posted there," says Marta.

ORGANIZE WHAT YOU'LL NEED AGAIN AND AGAIN

Every nonprofit marketer needs to get his or her hands on the same files over and over again. Get all that information together in one place. The following section details what you definitely need.

Get Clean Copies of Your Logo in the Proper Resolutions

It seems like not a day goes by that I don't see some raggedy, blurred, or skewed nonprofit logo on TV or in print that looks like it has been sent through a fax machine three times. Don't lift your logo off your website or from a word processing document and expect it to look good elsewhere.

Go find your original artwork files. They are most likely Adobe Illustrator or Photoshop files. Once you find those, add "original" to the filename so you know not to change these source files. Then make copies and start saving them in different formats and resolutions appropriate to various uses, putting "web" and "print" in the filenames to help you keep them straight.

For online use, the resolution should be 72 ppi (pixels per inch). So if you want your logo to appear as 1.5 inches square on your website, the dimensions would be 108 pixels by 108 pixels (that's 72 × 1.5). Save web resolution files as a .jpg, .gif, or .png. Use these on websites and blogs and in email.

For print use, the resolution should be at least 300 ppi. So your same 1.5 square-inch logo on a piece of paper would now be 450 × 450 pixels (300 × 1.5). Save these as eps or tiff files. You can also use a .jpg, but just make sure that the resolution and size are set high enough.

For TV, I recommend sending the highest-quality logo you have and letting the company you are working with adjust the size and resolution to match their needs.

If you can't find your original artwork files, get them redrawn. Either ask your graphic designer to do it or find a volunteer or college student who knows Adobe Illustrator. You'll need to know which fonts you used or be willing to have the designer take a guess. Unless your old logo is extremely complicated, it will probably take a designer about an hour to redraw it. The $100 to $200 you spend on this will pay for itself by making your organization look much more professional.

Gather Your Boilerplate Text

Put all of those chunks of text that you use over and over in one place. That includes your mission and vision statements, plain-English descriptions of your programs, your history, your elevator speeches, staff bios, press release boilerplate, organizational Frequently Asked Questions, and anything else that you find yourself frequently copying and pasting.

Start a Style Guide

Much time is wasted correcting inconsistencies in everything from your branding, which includes how staff use your logo, colors, or fonts, to which editorial styles you prefer (anyone want to argue about serial commas?). Spare yourself and everyone else who creates content for you the misery of these arguments by creating style guides for your organization.

An editorial style sheet is a chart you fill out showing how you will use, format, and spell certain words. You can also include rules about abbreviations, capitalization, acronyms, and anything else related to how words, numbers, and punctuation appear in your publications. Include anything and everything that you end up correcting when editing someone else's work. Here are some common decisions for your style sheet.

- When do you spell out numbers? Under 10 or under 100?
- Do you use periods in acronyms or not, such as USA or U.S.A.?
- Do you hyphenate certain words? For example, is it email or e-mail? Decision-maker or decision maker?
- Formatting phone numbers—use parentheses around the area code or not? Periods or hyphens in between segments?
- Formatting email addresses—all lower case, or are capital letters OK?
- Formatting website addresses—include the http:// and www. or not?

You should also create design style sheets that specify which fonts, colors, and other design elements you use, and when and where you use them.

Distribute your style guides widely and put them in places staff and volunteers can easily access, such as an electronic copy on your intranet or printed copies on an office bulletin board. Supplement the style guide with a running list of examples or answers to style questions raised by staff.

Track Supporter Data

Nonprofit communicators waste time when they can't find the data they need to connect with their supporters in the way they'd like to. Whether you use a simple database or spreadsheet or a more robust customer/constituent relationship management (CRM) package, you need to centralize your contact information and donation history for your supporters. Look at every form, both in print and online, in which your organization asks supporters for personal information, then ensure that the forms match up with the fields in your database. Establish and religiously implement a system for getting data that's collected offline into the database.

Data management has serious consequences, both positive and negative, for nonprofit marketers. Arts Corps, which brings artistic expression to young people in schools and community settings in the Seattle area, was tracking participant data, but not in ways that supported its marketing or programs. Class enrollment data was in one place, attendance data in another. They often had to pay a consultant to create reports they should have been able to generate on their own. They knew there had to be a better way, so they asked NPower Seattle, a nonprofit that helps others nonprofits with technology solutions, for advice.

In 2006, NPower helped Art Corps begin using Salesforce, a constituent relationship management database, to record student enrollment, track attendance, keep the online class calendar updated, and maintain donor records, all in one place.

"Those reports we used to struggle with became a snap to produce. The essential information we needed for operations and decision making, whether a mailing list or stats on program usage, were suddenly just a click away," says Leslie Collins, Arts Corps deputy director. Leslie believes that using the new database contributed to a 45 percent growth in student enrollment over two years by freeing up staff time to support programming. Because the database is now integrated with their website, people can find the information they need online. "That has greatly reduced the number of calls we take at the office, freeing up staff time and energy," says Leslie.

"It's amazing how the database and the web integration have enabled us to share information that then becomes part of the story of who we are and the difference we make in the community. Our donors and prospective donors can see the actual results of what we're doing," says Leslie. "We are a better, stronger organization today because of the work NPower did with us."

TRACK, TEST, AND DO WHAT WORKS

How do you know what works for your organization? You need to test and track. A 2007 survey by GettingAttention.org found that only 37 percent of nonprofits were tracking the effectiveness of their marketing campaigns. This is a real shame, because tracking is what helps you figure out what's working, what's not, and how you can be more effective long term, ultimately saving you a great deal of time.

Most online marketing tools have tracking built into them—you are already paying for them. You just have to use them.

Website tools. Any halfway decent hosting package will include a basic statistics package, or you can use Google Analytics for free. If you are particularly pressed for time and want to track only a few elements on a monthly basis, review these stats:

- *Visits or page views*—The number of people looking at each page. This tells you the most popular pages on your site.
- *Unique visitors*—How many different people are visiting your site, regardless of how many times they returned.
- *Referrers*—Where your visitors were before they came to your site. Are they finding you through Google, by typing in your URL directly, or by clicking on a link from someone else's site?
- *Click path*—Where people come into your site, where they go, and where they leave. You can also look at top entry and exit pages, but the full click path gives you a better sense for how people typically use your site.
- *Keywords*—Which words people are using in search engines to find your site (and conversely, which words are important to you that don't appear to be bringing people to your site).

Email newsletters. Your email newsletter service provider will provide data on what happens after they send out your email newsletters. Watch for trends in this data:

- *Released or sent successfully*—Your total list minus bounced messages. This helps you track the quality of your list over time. The fewer bounces, the better.
- *Open rate*—How many people are opening the email (HTML email only).
- *Click-throughs*—How many people are clicking on a link in the email. This shows they are reading it and taking action or looking for more information. You can also see which links they are clicking on.
- *Forwards*—How many people are forwarding your message to someone else.
- *Unsubscribes*—How many people are getting off your list. Don't be alarmed if you regularly lose a few people. But if your unsubscribes spike, carefully examine what in that particular message sent people fleeing from your list.

Blogs. Why are you blogging in the first place? The answer will determine what you should be tracking. In addition to the preceding statistics for websites, which also apply to blogs, also watch these statistics:

- *Subscribers*—How many people have affirmatively shown interest in your blog by subscribing to your RSS feed.
- *Discussion quality*—How many people are commenting on your posts, linking to them, or tweeting/retweeting them.

CONCLUSION: GIVE YOURSELF A BREAK

When I'm stuck on a problem, I do one of three things: take a walk, take a shower, or take a nap. Nearly every time, by physically removing myself from the problem and giving my brain a break, I find a creative solution.

I'm not alone. Neuroscientists who study how the human brain solves problems say that our ability to find those creative insights is related to whether we can find connections between seemingly disparate pieces.[1] Time away from a problem is a key element in finding those connections. Studies show that creative revelations often arise when our minds are busy with some unrelated task. Sleeping on a problem increases the likelihood that you'll solve it.

In the chaos of your daily life as a nonprofit marketer, remember that you'll actually be more creative—and therefore often more efficient—if you stop spending so much time focusing on a problem and give yourself a break.

chapter
FOURTEEN

Find the Talent: Keep Learning and Get Good Help

Help others achieve their dreams and you will achieve yours.

—Les Brown

This chapter is about . . .

- Your professional development as a nonprofit marketer
- Delegating marketing tasks to others
- Working with volunteers, interns, and freelancers

Marketing in the nonprofit world can mean different things to different people, which means your job description may vary significantly from someone with the same title at a nonprofit down the street. Do you write the newsletter? Do you have control over the website design? Are you responsible for fundraising? Are you the spokesperson for the nonprofit? Do you have a say in programmatic design and implementation decisions, or do program people work with you only when they need "outreach"?

No matter what exactly you are responsible for, nonprofit marketing requires a complicated skill set that's hard to find all in one person. It's a tough job.

In this chapter, we'll look at what you can do to build your own skills and how to delegate marketing tasks to others. We'll also look at empowering volunteers and hiring others to assist you. Get used to asking for help. You are going to need it.

EVERYONE ON STAFF IS A MARKETER (LIKE IT OR NOT)

Everyone talks about work when they're outside the office, so everyone on your staff is marketing your organization in one way or another. That's why it's so important that you keep everyone updated on both the strategies and the tactics you are using. Share everything from press releases and newsletters to direct mail appeals and Facebook updates with everyone on staff at the same time that these go public—and if possible, before they go public. That will be easier to do with press releases and newsletters than with Twitter updates, but the idea is to keep your native messengers up-to-date. If information overload is a problem or other staff just aren't interested in reading what you produce, create a short weekly briefing email and send it on Monday mornings to all staff so they know what's going out this week.

If you take the time to talk to staff members about how vital their role is in reaching out to your supporters, you may be surprised at the marketing skills you find in your midst. Are there any good writers, designers, or proofreaders on staff? Staff who seem to know everyone? People who know different software or social media sites inside-out? Sit down with the other staff and talk about what they are good at and how they would like to help you get the word out about the organization. Marketing can be scary for people who know nothing about it. You'll be perceived as an expert, whether you are or not. Be supportive, and look for ways that you can help program people, as you ask them to help you.

BUILD YOUR OWN SKILLS

While you look for help from within your organization, you should also look at ways to improve your own skill set. If you are a marketing department of one or a do-it-all-yourself executive director, it's especially important that you use as many of the following strategies as you can to develop your skills.

Try It on Your Own

Try something new. Get beyond your comfort zone. Experiment.

Figure out what you can learn on your own with some free (or cheap) tutorials online. Take an hour or two to work through the exercises. I'm also a big fan of using your children and pets as your personal guinea pigs. I blogged about my kids for our far-flung family and friends for a year before I started blogging professionally. My first photo and video uploads were of pets and kids. Play around for awhile at home before you try it at work.

Read Like Crazy

There's an incredible amount of assistance out there, especially with constantly changing technology and the ways in which marketers are using it, if you take the time to find it and read it. Schedule twenty minutes a day or an hour a week to close the door, turn off the phone, sit back, and read. Find and subscribe to the most helpful blogs. (You'll find my list of recommendations for nonprofit marketers on the companion website.) Read a book, like this one! Not everything you need to know can be found online. No time for reading? Listen instead to any of the great podcasts that several nonprofit marketing bloggers are producing (you'll find podcast recommendations on the companion website too).

Don't Cut Out Networking

There are times when you need to hunker down and get "it" done, whatever it is. But don't cut out networking. If you find the right group of smart, experienced people to hang out with, they will save you incredible amounts of time. It's healthy for both you and your organization for you to mix and mingle with people who understand the work you do but who aren't working on the exact same thing day in and day out. You'll make new connections, pick up some tips, and get some great advice.

Build Training into Your Work Plan and Budget

You can learn only so much on your own. Many opportunities will be free, but you'll need to fill in the gaps with paid training. Outline what you need to learn how to do, why, and how much it will cost. Identify the training you need most and justify it. C'mon, you are in marketing, so market the need for that training budget! Explain how your productivity and results will change as a result of learning a new skill. Webinars are a great way to get professional training without spending money on travel. See the companion website for a list of who offers affordable webinars on nonprofit marketing, communications, and fundraising.

LEARN TO EDIT YOUR OWN WORK

If you are a communications department of one, that often means you have to edit your own work. Here are several suggestions for editing your own copy so it appears that you have a full staff of editors at your disposal.

Cut the first few sentences. Lots of people (including me) need to warm up as they start writing and don't really get to the point until a few sentences in. Warming up is good for working out, but not for writing at work. Pinpoint the first sentence where you get to the point, and delete those unnecessary preliminary sentences.

Jettison the background information. We often assume that people need more history than they really do. Sum up any critical background in one sentence and tell the readers where to find additional background or to contact you if they need it.

Focus on what you want from the reader. Are you expecting the reader to take a particular action based on your memo or whatever it is you are writing? If so, focus your draft on that. What do you want them to do? Why should they do it? How should they do it? Cut everything else that doesn't contribute to moving that reader to action.

Watch for tangents. It's easy to stray from the main point. Watch for tangents and babbling streams of consciousness. Turn those sections of your draft into separate memos or articles.

Cut the wordy phrases, redundancies, clichés, and so on. Shorter is better. Cut out all the words that don't contribute to your meaning.

Watch for unnecessary details. Too much detail can overwhelm readers, and too much text can make it impossible for your supporters to skim your writing (which is what most of them want to do). Define the one thing you want people to remember and really focus on that. In email and web copy, use links to provide all the details and tangential information.

Read it out loud, then cut any parts you read quickly or skipped over. If you find yourself zooming through sections when you read something out loud, it likely means that section isn't that important and can be edited out.

Take a long break. The easiest way to convince your brain that it is reading something new is to put some time between your original writing and your editing. Waiting a day or two is best, but even a couple of hours will help. Do something that doesn't involve the written word (file that big pile of paper on your desk or make some phone calls). If you must continue to write or read, work on a topic that's unrelated to the material you need to edit.

Print it out. If you wrote your document on a computer, change the medium for editing and print it out. It may seem like a waste of time to make your changes on paper and again online, but you're much more likely to produce an error-free document that way.

Change the background. If you prefer to edit online or don't have immediate access to a printer, you can still make the document look completely different to your eyes. For example, try changing the background color of the document. In Microsoft Word, go to "Format" then "Background" to change the color. This changes the color of your document on the screen only.

DELEGATE MARKETING TASKS TO OTHERS

No matter how dedicated to your cause you may be, you are still human, and there are only so many hours in the day. Decide what only you can do and what you can ask others to do, even if it means you have to accept that they may approach the task in a different way. Delegate what you can, especially tasks that are too easy for you (meaning someone else who is probably paid less than you can do it) as well as tasks that are too hard for you (meaning you can pay for someone else's expertise and get the job done much more quickly). Look for opportunities to train others to help you, and be willing to let go of control enough so that they can.

Before you can find others to help you, you should have some sense for what you need them to do. Content creation is an obvious place to start. Ask someone to be a guest columnist for ongoing publications like your newsletters, blog, and website. Find volunteers who are into writing, design, photography, and videography. Can they create templates for you or set up social media accounts? Does your table-top display for conferences and fairs need to be updated?

Research is another time-consuming task that can be done by others. Ask volunteers or consultants to interview and write up stories about your clients and donors. Ask them to research which reporters in your area are covering various types of stories to update your press list. Ask them to collect bids for print jobs or event catering. Match your needs with what your volunteers genuinely enjoy doing.

Do you have a volunteer with an analytical mind? Ask them to dive into your website and email newsletter stats to identify positive and negative trends and to look for hidden gems of information you can use to improve your marketing program.

After other staff, the most obvious place to turn for help is your board of directors. Who on your board of directors has skills that can help you? Board members aren't likely to actually do the work for you long term, but they may be able to put you in touch with great contacts who can make your work life much easier. Board members can also offer perspectives you may be missing on staff. They may also be willing to invest time to help you get your systems set up, such as creating templates for an email newsletter or suggesting new strategies to reach particular target audiences.

Next, look for supportive volunteers who are interested in working with your cause because they care. Come up with some substantive projects that you can supervise, but that you don't have time to do yourself. Volunteers should be able to see the impact of their work, or to at least understand how it helps make your organization work more smoothly.

EMPOWER VOLUNTEERS SO THEY'LL COME BACK AGAIN

Time is precious—more precious than money in some ways—and that's what volunteers are giving you. You want to get something out of your volunteers, and they want to get something out of the experience too. Never forget that. Here are some key principles for ensuring that your volunteers will want to keep volunteering for you:

- *Set clear expectations.* If volunteers are creating content for you, spell out the approval process so they understand that you may ask them to make changes. Explain how what you are asking them to create fits into your larger content creation strategy. Give them a sense for the type of feedback they can expect from you.
- *Assume they'll get it right.* Don't hover. Be supportive by asking if they have questions or need help, but otherwise assume that your volunteers are smart,

capable, and responsible people who will do their best for you. If they do get it wrong, be positive by pointing out what is right and gently moving on to areas that need to be changed. Always end the conversation on a positive note, expressing your gratitude for their help.

- *Be flexible.* You need to make sure that what your volunteers are doing is something you need done. At the same time, don't be too prescriptive. Offer some flexibility in how the work gets done. This is especially true in areas where style and quality can be highly subjective, like writing and design. Acknowledge your own style. As you edit an article, try not to replace your volunteer's personal style with your own. Also know the differences between rules and questions of style. Before you make lots of changes to your volunteer's words, be sure you can clearly explain which corrections are essential and which are optional. Your editorial style sheet will come in handy here!
- *Let them do what they love.* As much as possible, match tasks to what volunteers really enjoy doing. Your best volunteers will be those who are excited about the work and feel like they are personally gaining something from the experience.
- *Thank them, and thank them again.* Share your gratitude for the help often. Remember, without them, either you'd be doing the work late at night or it wouldn't get done at all. Always remind your volunteers how important they are and about the real difference they are making.

HIRING INTERNS FOR SOCIAL MEDIA PROJECTS

Follow these tips to ensure that both you and your interns are happy with the experience.

1. *Make it a team effort, led by the intern.* Social media is—well, social. And that's why it holds so much promise for nonprofits. You can connect with friends of friends of friends you might not otherwise reach. But the organization needs to be at the center of this network, not some intern who is leaving in three months. The intern can lead the way and set everything up, but permanent staff, long-time volunteers, and board members must be a part of it too. The team approach also gives your intern valuable project

and team management experience, so she isn't just sitting alone in front of a computer.

2. *Be clear about why you are doing it.* "Getting on YouTube" is not a marketing goal. Who are you trying to reach and with what message? What do you want these new friends you'll make to do? Why is getting on Facebook or YouTube the right tactic? Know the answers to these questions ahead of time so that your intern and the team can create a presence online that complements your existing communications work.
3. *Make training a part of the assignment—and you get schooled.* For your social media project to succeed, the senior management of your organization needs to understand it. Even if you as the executive director or development director don't log in every day, you still need to understand the culture and vocabulary of the site, what people actually do there, and how your organization is being represented. Give your intern at least fifteen minutes every two weeks to show you and other senior managers what he or she is doing online and to give you some quick lessons on how you can do it yourself.
4. *Open your mind.* If the only way you can see your nonprofit getting onto social media sites is by asking a younger person to do it for you, there's a good chance that you don't fully understand what it's all about and just why "everybody's doing it" in the first place. For example, you may not be entirely comfortable with the idea that other people (those friends of friends you covet) may be talking about *your* organization and *your* issues in their own words, ignoring your talking points and failing to keep all the facts straight.

   This is where you have to remember that social media is not about pushing information out, but about conversations about the information you share and collaboration that grows out of those conversations. Relax and go with it. Gently correct when it's really important to do so. Thank your new friends for caring. You may be pleasantly surprised at the new ideas and insights you discover.

HIRE CONSULTANTS AND FREELANCERS

When you don't have the important, creative skills you need on staff to accomplish your nonprofit marketing program, look for affordable freelancers and consultants to fill in the gaps. Ask yourself these seven questions before you hire a freelancer creative professional, like a writer, editor, graphic artist, or designer.

Before you start interviewing . . .

1. *What do I want a freelancer to do?* The more specific you can be about what you need, the better you'll be able to recruit a freelancer who can meet your needs. Most writers think in terms of word count or page count when estimating a job, so you should think that way too. How much writing do you need? How much research or interviewing will the writer need to do? How many drafts do you typically want to see?

2. *What is my ideal deadline, and what is the* real *deadline?* Most people want projects they are hiring out to be completed yesterday. Although it's fine to suggest an ideal deadline when soliciting proposals from freelancers, know in your own mind how much play you have in your schedule. If the perfect candidate comes along, but can't meet your ideal deadline, for whatever reason, do you have enough cushion in your schedule to hire that person anyway?

3. *How much do I have to spend?* Rates for freelancers vary widely. In some respects you do get what you pay for, but even among highly qualified and experienced freelancers you will still find a great deal of variability in rates. Know how much you have to spend ahead of time, so when you begin to evaluate proposals you can eliminate those that are far beyond your means. At the same time, you should also strongly consider eliminating proposals that seem exceedingly low—it's a hallmark of an inexperienced freelancer to charge way below market rate.

As you are interviewing . . .

4. *Is this freelancer a good listener?* Equally important as creative skills are the ability to listen to your needs and incorporate them into the project. Your projects will include many variables, such as audience, message, and tone, all of which require that you and the freelancer work together to get it right. You should treat this relationship as a partnership, which requires that you both listen well.

5. *Does this freelancer seem flexible?* Much of marketing is subjective. While some elements, such as correct grammar and word count, are objective, whether the piece meets your needs in terms of style is highly subjective.

A good freelancer knows this and will work with you to get the style the way you want it, even if the first draft is way off.

Also, as the project progresses, you may very well change your mind about how you want an issue handled or what elements should be emphasized. Try to gauge whether the freelancer can "go with the flow" and adjust accordingly. Of course, you need to be willing to pay for extra drafts if you change the scope of work significantly.

6. *Do I like this freelancer's portfolio and client list?* Does the freelancer have experience with your type of project? Does the freelancer's list of clients relate to your organization in subject area, size, or some other meaningful measure? All professional freelancers should be able to provide samples of their work (many will have online portfolios for you to peruse) and to give you a list of people they have worked for previously.
7. *How do this freelancer's other clients describe their relationships?* Yes, you should check references. Speaking directly with another client is one of the best ways to judge how well a freelancer works with clients. Pick up the phone and call. Ask how many jobs the person has given to the freelancer. Repeat business is always a good sign.

CONCLUSION: KNOW WHEN YOU NEED HELP—AND ASK FOR IT

In an ideal world, if you were marketing your nonprofit organization on your own, you would be a good writer and designer (or have an eye for good and bad designs created by others). You would understand how people like your supporters get their information, and how reading print is very different from reading online. You would study psychology, so you would understand what motivates people, including your donors and other supporters, but also your board of directors and partners. You would have a little bit of tech geek in you, accidental or otherwise, to appreciate how online tools work and work together (or not). You would know how to juggle many tasks and deadlines. You would manage others in ways that inspire them to be as productive and creative as possible, without burning them out.

But you're not living in an ideal world, are you? In your very real world, you can see that it's impossible for any one person to do all of these things well. So don't be too hard on yourself. Find others who can help you get it all done.

chapter FIFTEEN

Find the Treasure: Market Your Good Cause on a Tight Budget

He who knows how to be poor knows everything.

—Jules Michelet

This chapter is about . . .

- **Applying triage to your marketing to-do list**
- **Shifting more of your marketing online**
- **Where to spend and where to scrimp**

At some point in your nonprofit marketing career, you've probably found yourself in one of these three situations:

- You realized how important marketing is, but didn't have a budget to support it.
- You always had a marketing program, but the budget for it just got slashed.
- You were told you needed to find ways to raise money to cover communications expenses.

All three situations can be addressed by following the strategies in this chapter, including focusing in on what's most important and forgoing the rest, taking a more friendly and casual approach to your marketing, and shifting more of your marketing online. We'll also look at where to spend and where to scrimp when money is tight.

DON'T RATTLE YOUR TIP CUP

Even when your organization is struggling, you should always keep your communications focused on your cause and the people you serve, not on your organization per se. Don't make it about you and how your agency is hurting. Make it about the good work you are trying to do, the people you are trying to serve, and how much your supporters are needed.

People want to feel like they are giving to an organization that's healthy and that makes a difference. They want to be part of your success, not your failure. If all of your messaging is about how you're having trouble paying your utility bills and how you may close your doors any minute, you'll breed more skepticism about your management abilities than confidence in your ability to make a difference. Focus on the impact your supporters can have on the people you're helping and on your cause, not the plight of your organization.

MARKETING TRIAGE: FOCUS IN AND FORGET THE REST

When your resources are limited, you have to make choices. In Chapter Four, we discussed how you must forget the general public and focus in on the people who matter most to your success. When money is tight, it's even more important to go through the process of creating audience groups and personas, then focus specifically on those people. You don't have the luxury of doing general outreach, public education, or awareness raising through the eyes and ears of just anyone you might happen to reach. Instead, you need to focus in—and there are several ways to get there.

The RFM model. RFM stands for *recency, frequency, and monetary value.* This is a common model in retail sales, but you can also apply it to how your list of supporters interacts with you. Recency looks at the last time a person took an action related to your organization, whether donating money, volunteering time, or opening your e-newsletter. The more recently a person took an action, the more likely that person will do it again. The same goes for frequency. How often has a supporter donated to you in the last year or how many times have they volunteered or clicked on links in your newsletter? If they frequently do any of these things, they are more likely to continue to do them. Monetary value measures the size of their gifts of money or time to you. If you need to cut back on the number of people you are communicating with, you can use the RFM model to figure out who should stay on the list and who you can put on hold. You can also use it to put certain people at the top of the list for special, personal attention.

By interests. If you are cutting back your communications budget, odds are that you are cutting back in other programmatic areas as well. Perhaps you used to operate five different programs and now you can operate only three. If your database of supporters includes information about who is interested or involved in which program, you can cut back communications with the people who were most interested in the programs you are no longer operating. In an ideal world you might try to move these people over to the other programs you continue to maintain, but if you are performing triage on your list, they are likely candidates for cutting.

Your VIPs. Every organization has a circle of Very Important People—important to your success, that is. Even if you decide that you must eliminate communications to your mailing list, you must still find a way to stay in touch with your VIPs. In addition to your major individual donors, don't overlook your grant and contract managers. Nonprofits will often overlook the program officer at the foundation or the bureaucrat at the government agency who manages the grant or contract paperwork, unless it's time to turn in a report or cash a check. Those people, however, have a lot of influence over whether you'll receive additional support in the future—and how much it will be. Be sure to keep them in the loop. Even though they represent organizational sources of money, treat these people like individual donors. Even if you eliminate your newsletter, be sure to send all of your VIPs occasional emails or personal letters updating them on your work.

Calls to action. Another way to focus in is to look at not who is on your list, but the communications you send them. Analyze the content of all of your communications; if you need to cut back on quantity to save money, make sure the remaining communications pieces focus on very clear calls to action. Know exactly why you are communicating and what you want the person on the other end to do as a result of that communication. Minimize or eliminate entirely the general "FYI" outreach. If you are always asking people to do something, you run the risk of being seen as pushy. It's nice to provide information and helpful resources to your supporters without asking for anything in return. But if the budget axe is falling, focus on calls to action that can produce results, whether it's more volunteer hours, event registrations, or donations.

Jeff Brooks, writer of the Future Fundraising Now blog, suggests you look at it this way: Would you rather move a hundred people 10 percent of the way toward giving to your cause or move ten people 100 percent of the way toward giving? When you have a nice healthy budget that you can count on year after year, moving a hundred people 10 percent of the way is a valid goal, because you are putting people in the pipeline for gifts in later years. But in perilous times, when your organization's very survival may be in question, moving ten people all the way toward giving is going to be a much better approach for your organization. That requires extreme focus on very specific people, at the exclusion of others.

GO CASUAL AND FRIENDLY

Forget the twelve-page print newsletter and the twenty-page annual report. Forget the fundraising gala. They are too expensive. Instead, go friendly and casual. Many of your supporters will appreciate a more relaxed approach, whether you do it for financial reasons or not!

Make phone calls and send email. Unless your supporters are spread out across the land and you have a terrible long-distance plan, calling them every now and then will be much cheaper than sending them print mail. Also send personal emails—not just your e-newsletter that's sent out to everyone, but personal emails directly from you and specifically to one of your supporters. Keep both calls and emails brief and limited to one primary purpose.

Call or email to say thank you. Call or email to share a story about your work. Call or email to tell them about a fun event you think they'd enjoy, even if your group isn't the one hosting it.

This leads to the question: do you call or email? Ideally, you know which each supporter prefers, because you've asked and are keeping track of these and other preferences.

Use these five-minute conversations to learn more about what your supporters care about, what they are interested in, and why they think your cause is so great. This is information that you need in order to cultivate that relationship long term, regardless of your financial conditions, but especially when times are tough.

Write handwritten notes. If you are cutting back on your budget, it's likely that your donors are cutting back on their personal budgets too. Which nonprofits will stay at the top of their lists? The ones with whom they feel the most personal connection.

As a board member for a local group, I was asked to write personal notes on the top of several fundraising appeal letters. At the top of a letter to a woman I knew, I wrote something like, "Hello Anne: Now that I'm serving on this board, I really see how much help our neighbors need. Thanks so much for being there for them. I'll hope you'll consider a generous gift this year, too—Kivi."

When I ran into Anne a few weeks later, she said she had a bone to pick with me. I was nervous until she said, "I had planned to stop giving to that organization because I needed to trim back this year. But when I saw your note, I had to put them back on my list." She ended with a smile and a faux-sarcastic "Thanks a lot!" Anne gave a bigger gift than she had the year before to an organization she had planned to cut off entirely. The personal touch really does work, not all of the time with everyone, but many times with enough people to make the extra effort worthwhile.

Make your events casual. Make your events more casual, personal experiences. People associate backyard barbecues and house parties with their friends, and you want to be included in that group. They associate big galas with wealth, and if you don't have money, you can't afford to throw that kind of event. When times are tough, many people don't want to be seen at lavish, over-the-top events anyway. Consumer trends show that people are craving personal, friendly, and casual experiences with people they know, like, and trust. Give your supporters what they want.

This kind of approach also translates into the auction items you request for your fundraisers. Instead of asking people to donate expensive vacations, jewelry, artwork, or other luxury items, ask them to donate special experiences instead. For example, you can ask a chef at a local restaurant to offer cooking lessons or to name a weekly special on the menu after the highest bidder.

MORE FRIENDLY, AFFORDABLE BROCHURE NETS MORE SUPPORTERS AND DONATIONS

Kelly Stettner, director of the Black River Action Team (BRAT) in Springfield, Vermont, wasn't happy with her organization's brochure. "It was pretty—full of clip art and fancy fonts—yet bland," says Kelly. When it was time to redesign the brochure, Kelly eliminated a lot of unnecessary text, simplified the fonts and colors, included testimonials from volunteers, and added action photos of people working on BRAT projects. At the same time, she added more white space and simplified the layout to work very well in black-and-white.

"By showing actual volunteers performing actual projects, the brochures catch more attention and almost fly off my booth. In addition, by using simple black-and-white printing and inexpensive paper, I am demonstrating that we use donations frugally and have our priorities straight," says Kelly. "I'm seeing a slow but steady increase in volunteerism as well as donations. Personal stories and photos combined with streamlined, economical savvy make a big difference in people's opinions of my group!"

UNFAMILIAR WITH SOME OF THE TERMS IN THIS CHAPTER?

If you find some of the terminology in this section foreign or confusing, refer to the Glossary of Online Marketing Terms at the back of the book.

SHIFT YOUR MARKETING FROM PRINT TO PIXELS

When you ask nonprofits what their biggest marketing expenses are, most will give you answers related to something they send out in the mail. It's not just the postage; it's the graphic design and printing, along with delivery, that make printed newsletters, annual reports, and direct mail campaigns so expensive.

Online marketing costs pennies on the print dollar. Using email more effectively is the best way to eliminate dollars in your print budget. Next, spend some time on your search engine optimization and marketing. This replaces money you may be spending on print advertising. Instead, make sure that your website comes up when people search on topics related to your work in Google or Bing. After setting up your email communications and ensuring that your site is optimized for search engines, consider adding a blog. Finally, look at how you can use social media, including video- and photo-sharing sites and social networking sites like Facebook and LinkedIn.

Should you eliminate your print newsletter? For many nonprofits, this is the single biggest marketing expense and therefore a vexing question. To make this decision, go back to your audience. Are they likely to sit down and read your newsletter cover to cover? Do they get most of their information through the mail or from print sources like magazines and newspapers? Do they want to receive a newsletter from you? Is that the best way for you to spread your message to them? Is the newsletter more than paying for itself, based on the donations that are returned in the envelopes inserted in the newsletter?

For decades, a print newsletter has been the default communications tactic for a nonprofit organization. That should no longer be the case. Instead, you should carefully analyze your audience and your marketing goals and determine whether print or email, or some combination of the two, is the most appropriate channel. Perhaps print would work better for a smaller segment of your list, with everyone else receiving email. After all, you can affordably print short runs of a newsletter on a copier.

If you can't decide, go with email. It's not only more cost-effective, but it's also more timely, more conversational (assuming you monitor the reply-to address), and more participatory (readers can click on links to learn more and take action). Only after going through the process of analyzing your audience, your message, and your best communications tactics should you decide to use a print newsletter.

SWITCHING FROM A PRINT NEWSLETTER TO AN EMAIL NEWSLETTER

If you decide that the pros of emailing your newsletter to your supporters outweigh the cons and you are ready to make the transition from print to email, follow these ten tips.

1. *Don't try the short-cuts.* Sending a PDF of your print newsletter out as an attachment to an email list is not an email newsletter. Neither is sending a one-line email that says, "Click here to read our newsletter on our website." If you are going to use email to communicate regularly with your supporters, you'll need to create a real e-newsletter, with real content in the email itself. You also need to send it out using an email newsletter service provider. Don't send it out from your desktop email program. The benefits of using an email marketing company far exceed the minimal monthly costs.

   The Blue Dragon Children's Foundation based in Hanoi, Vietnam, tried sending its e-newsletter by attaching a PDF file to an email sent via its Gmail account. Not only was this extremely time consuming, but staff had no way to deal with bouncing email addresses and people who wanted to unsubscribe. "We did it all by hand," says Amy Cherry, the foundation's communications manager. "With a small, already overworked staff, newsletter time drove us crazy. We had no idea how many people were getting it, opening it, or reading it."

After researching how other organizations were doing their email newsletters, Amy realized the foundation was doing it all wrong. They signed up with an email newsletter service provider, and the positive results were immediate. "We have loads more time. No more dealing with the headache of sending out the email through Gmail. And the coolest part is that we are now able to track how many people read the newsletter, and we've organized our donors into different email lists so we can track them better," says Amy. Mailing list management, including unsubscribes, is now automated, and the e-newsletter sign-up box on their website connects directly to the mailing list database. "It's the best thing we've done," says Amy.

2. *Dissect your old print newsletter.* Not everything that you included in your print newsletter will be right for your email newsletter. For example, if you had a large calendar of events in print, it's best to highlight only a few events in an email newsletter, with links to a full calendar on your website. Think about what belongs where online—not everything will work in an email.
3. *Skip the letter from the director.* Honestly, these are often ghastly in print because they are typically full of jargon and behind-the-scenes minutiae, all of which is exactly opposite of what works in email. If the director really loves writing that letter, then it's time to give him or her a blog. Your email newsletter, on the other hand, should be focused primarily on the readers and what they care about and how they can connect to you and your cause. Very brief letters can work, but they must be laser-focused on the reader—the letter is simply a format for content you want to share, not an open invitation for the director to ramble.
4. *Consider a more personal tone.* Email is a more personal form of communication than print. If you've been writing your newsletter articles in the third person ("The Dog Lovers' Association is seeking volunteers"), now is the time to move to a more personal first person–second person style ("If you'd like to volunteer to walk dogs, we want to hear from you").

5. *Practice writing five-hundred-word articles.* Articles in email newsletters should be much shorter than what you typically see in print. Shoot for no more than five hundred words. If you need to go longer, include an excerpt in the email and have readers click over to your website to read the full article.
6. *Decide on full text, teasers, or a combo.* An email newsletter should be relatively short compared to a print newsletter. That means you have to make some decisions about the quantity and length of articles. Some organizations will include one full article in an email newsletter, with headlines only for other articles that appear only on a website. Others will include teaser text or longer blurbs for all of the articles, requiring readers to click over to the website for the full version of each article. Either way is acceptable, but I think it's best to be consistent from issue to issue.
7. *Prepare to spend lots of time on microtext.* Working on the microtext like headings and captions is important in print, but it's absolutely essential in email. Start working now on the kinds of subject lines, headlines, and subheads you'll use in your email newsletter. A large portion of your mailing list members will quickly skim and read only the microtext, so make it good.
8. *Get as many email addresses as you can.* Warn your print newsletter readers repeatedly that you are transitioning into a new email format and make it easy for them to give you their email addresses. You'll need to create a mini–marketing campaign for the e-newsletter itself by emphasizing all the timely information and other benefits that your supporters will receive when they subscribe.
9. *Add a sign-up box to your website.* Ideally, this will appear in your site template so the sign-up box appears on every page of your website. At a minimum, put it on your Home page and your About Us or Contact Us pages. One of the benefits of using an email service provider is that your supporters can add themselves to your list automatically—but only if they can find the form on your website.
10. *Learn about your new metrics.* Email newsletter service providers will give you many more ways to measure the impact of your email newsletter than you ever had for print. Learn what those metrics are and how you can use them over time to improve your newsletter.

HOW TO MAKE YOUR REMAINING PRINT MARKETING MORE AFFORDABLE

Digital printing technology is changing fast, which means that printing small numbers of brochures or newsletters is much more affordable than it used to be. If you decide that you still want to send a print newsletter or other print communications using traditional offset printing, consider these steps to reduce your printing costs.

Ask your printer to recommend changes. One of the best untapped resources for lowering your print budget is your printing provider. Call up your account representative at your printer and tell him or her that you are considering dropping the newsletter entirely because of the expense of producing it (you won't be the only one). Explain that you would like to keep sending it out, but you need to make some changes to make it more affordable. Ask for suggested changes to the type of printing press, paper, format, length, inks, and so on that could bring down the price. Most printers will jump on this right away; if they don't, take copies of your current newsletter to other competitive print shops and see what they'd suggest.

Reduce the size. Paper is a large portion of your printing costs, so cutting the number of pages and reducing the size of the pages can significantly reduce your printing bill. The pieces of paper that are run through the printing press are much larger than what you end up with in your hands. Reducing the finished size of your publication by as little as a half-inch can change the way your individual pages are arranged on those bigger sheets of paper, which means you have to pay for fewer of those big sheets. Changing the size of your document can also reduce your mailing costs. If your printer is also your mail house, ask for revised mailing estimates as well.

The Montshire Museum of Science in Norwich, Vermont, is saving more than $1,000 per edition of its print newsletter, thanks to some small changes. They redesigned their quarterly print newsletter from an eight-page, 9 × 11.75 format to an eight-page, 6 × 11 format. The smaller size saves the museum money on postage and design fees, as well as staff time. "We have received a lot of positive comments about the new size. And I can use the $4,000 I'm saving each year for advertising, interns, photo shoots, or web design," says Beth Krusi, the museum's director of marketing and communications.

Use thinner, off-white paper. Changing the weight of the paper (how thick it feels) and the brightness of the paper (how white it is) can sometimes reduce the cost. Even if the price difference is small, it can add up over time. Just how white does the paper need to be, especially if you are covering it mostly with text? And just how heavy should each sheet feel in your hands? The brighter the white and the heavier a sheet of paper is, the more expensive the paper will usually be. One cost-effective approach for annual reports or other larger documents is to use a heavier, more expensive paper for the cover to give the document the right look and feel, but to use a more affordable house sheet of paper for the insides.

Don't be too picky about colors. The more colors you use in traditional offset printing, the more expensive your print job will be. Even if you decide to print in full color, you can still reduce your expenses by printing strictly in a four-color process, rather than requesting full color plus specific PMS colors. Instead, convert all of your PMS colors to their CMYK equivalent. You can use the Pantone Color Bridge to see the differences in the colors using the two different processes.

In my experience, the only time this has been a real issue was when a nonprofit was working with a corporate sponsor that insisted their logo appear in certain PMS colors. Depending on the actual colors, conversion to PMS may not be a big deal, and the sponsor may be just fine with that. But if they insist on the additional PMS colors, you may want to consider asking that sponsor to cover the cost difference, if it really is a significant increase in cost.

Prepare your files correctly. The further along in the printing process that you get, the more expensive it is to make changes. Make sure your documents are proofread several times and approved by everyone who needs to see them well before you send them to the printer. Also ensure that you have prepared your digital files properly for your printer. It's not as simple as handing over the file from the computer program you used to create the document. You'll also need to supply copies of fonts and high-resolution images. Another common problem is using the wrong or mixed color profiles. (Don't know the difference between RGB and CMYK? Talk to your printer or a graphic designer before submitting your files to a printer.) When your printer has to fix any of these problems with your files, you get billed for them.

POSTCARDS: A MORE AFFORDABLE APPROACH TO PRINT COMMUNICATIONS

To save money on their print newsletter, some nonprofits have resorted to sending it out to their mailing list only twice a year. My response: what's the point?

Updating your supporters twice a year on your work is not often enough to keep them engaged in what you do and top of mind when they consider contributing time or money. And each edition of a print newsletter typically costs thousands to print and mail, not including staff time. I question whether the newsletter is worth doing at all if you can do it only twice a year.

Instead of spending all that money to contact your supporters just twice, with questionable impact, consider switching to postcards. Naturally, every situation is different, but in many cases, a full-color postcard will cost about one-third of what a typical four-page color newsletter will cost to print and mail to your list. That means you could contact your supporters six times a year, instead of just twice, for the same money.

Postcards are a great marketing tactic for other reasons too. They are much more likely to be read than newsletters, because they fit right in with the way we all sort and read our mail today. In the few seconds we each give a piece of mail in the pile, a postcard can grab our hearts with a great photo (that graphic side is really important), deliver the key point we need to know, and motivate us to take the next step. Running a printed postcard campaign in conjunction with an email newsletter is a smart way to take advantage of both communications channels in an affordable and effective way.

WHERE TO SPEND YOUR LIMITED DOLLARS AND WHERE TO SCRIMP

Where should you spend the marketing dollars you do have? Start with these five categories of essential expenses.

Email newsletter service provider. You can't distribute your email newsletter out of your own desktop email program for a variety of reasons. You really do need to use an email newsletter or email marketing service. For about $30 per month, you can get a full-service account that provides everything you'll need to effectively use email to stay in touch with your supporters. Many services also include extras like built-in survey tools.

Digital cameras. Telling your story becomes so much easier when you have the right visuals. Buy both a digital camera for still photos and a digital video camera for video. The cost has dropped dramatically, and if you are primarily using photos and video online (meaning you don't need high-resolution images all the time), you have many affordable options available. You can find decent digital cameras and video recorders for under $200 each. Basic editing software will come with your camera.

Professional design and photography. It's important to present a professional image, yet many nonprofit websites, newsletters, and brochures look as though they were cobbled together by amateurs using the free software, templates, and imagery that every other person with a computer also owns. Hire a graphic designer to spruce up your templates or to design new ones just for you. Make it clear that you'll need to produce the actual pieces themselves, so you need a template that's easy to fill in yourself.

Likewise, consider hiring a professional photographer to capture the perfect images for your marketing. Great photos of real people working with your organization on its mission are incredibly valuable. Use photos on your website, in your email newsletters, and on your social networking sites. Although you can often find good options in photo-sharing sites like Flickr or through stock photography houses, it's hard to find that perfect image that says exactly what you need it to say. Explain your needs to an experienced professional photographer and you'll often be amazed at what you get back.

That's what TransForm, a San Francisco Bay Area advocate of public transportation and walkable communities, discovered. "All of the photos we were using in our communications were terrible: low quality, very amateur, not interesting. We had lots of bad pictures of buses and trains with the occasional back of someone's head getting on the bus or train," says Marta Lindsey, TransForm's communications and development director.

"We were about to launch a new website and realized that it wouldn't look good if we didn't invest in some better photographs. Looking at other websites, huge and gorgeous images are all over the best websites now," says Marta. TransForm decided to hire a professional photographer to capture the kinds of photo they needed to tell their story well.

Now they have fantastic images that show people walking, biking, and taking public transportation. "With just this one small and relatively affordable change, we immediately and dramatically improved our marketing and are using these new photos in multiple ways. The photos are doing the work for us by helping people understand what we do and how our work impacts real people," says Marta. "This has to be some of the best money we've spent on marketing."

Professional development. Because you are implementing much if not all of your marketing program on your own, you are going to need to learn many new skills. Figure out where your biggest skill gap is and fill it with either an affordable webinar or a how-to book. If you wish you could make minor tweaks to your website design, you might need an introductory class in HTML or PHP. If you are taking and sharing lots of photos, you might want to take a Photoshop course. If you have little experience with writing for the web and email, take an online writing webinar. You'll find many affordable training courses and webinars online. The money you spend learning new skills will save you many hours of frustration and will also save your organization from having to hire freelancers or consultants to solve minor problems.

LOOKING FOR THE BEST FREE MARKETING TOOLS FOR NONPROFITS?

For a list of my favorite free services for nonprofit marketers, visit the companion website.

Now, what are the nonessential marketing areas in which you can scrimp? Here are the first places I would look to eliminate expenditures:

- *Advertising.* Unless you have data that proves that paid advertising works for you, don't spend money on print or online ads. Focus on search engine optimization instead and apply for a Google Grant, which gives you free search advertising credits.
- *Fancy, splashy graphics.* Skip the Flash intro for your website and logos for individual programs. Focus your design resources on your overall branding, like your logo and website and newsletter templates.
- *Print mailings.* Carefully review what you are mailing out and consider cutting anything that isn't directly producing revenue and/or actions that are important to your organization (like taking advocacy actions or signing up to volunteer).
- *Donor premiums.* A handwritten thank-you letter will always be more valuable to your donors than gifts like pins, mugs, and T-shirts.

FUNDING YOUR NONPROFIT MARKETING PROGRAM

Marketing or communications programs are often the first to go in tight times, because short-sighted and highly stressed nonprofit decision makers don't consider them mission-critical. Most nonprofits pay for their nonprofit marketing programs out of their unrestricted funding, which also makes them a target when mission-oriented program are being cut.

Few foundation and government funders explicitly fund communications and marketing. Those that fund "capacity building" activities will often allow marketing and communications line items in grant proposals, especially if you clearly explain how your communications programs will help improve your organizational sustainability by building a community of loyal supporters around your cause.

You should always include communications in your programmatic, mission-oriented grant applications. As discussed throughout this book, good nonprofit marketing is really about community building. Discuss communications as a critical tactic in implementing the programmatic goal in your grant applications. You may need to describe your marketing line items in more traditional language that foundation funders are more comfortable with, such as "outreach" or "education." Corporate sponsors are more likely to understand the value of "marketing" and "communications" and to be more comfortable with that language.

CONCLUSION: ZERO COMMUNICATIONS BUDGET = ZERO SUSTAINABILITY

Your nonprofit marketing program is like a tree. It takes a long time to grow into something durable and dependable—something sustainable—that produces new supporters and keeps current ones happy year after year. Some years are better than others. Branches may break off now and then, and you need to prune away dead wood occasionally so other branches can grow stronger. You may even nip some new shoots off to direct their nutrients where they are most needed.

But never cut down the tree entirely, because once you do, it's gone. Don't cut your marketing budget entirely, even when times are tough. Prune the tree, yes, but never chop it down. Trees take far too long to grow from seeds or regenerate from stumps. If you completely ax your marketing program right now, you will feel the impact next year and for years to come. Long after your budget crunch is over, you'll still be sweating it out under the hot sun, while the other nonprofits who maintained their communications programs are sitting comfortably in the shade.

That's because nonprofit marketing is ultimately all about staying in touch with people and creating long-term relationships. When you stop talking to your friends, soon you are no longer friends. When you fail to communicate with your supporters, before long they no longer support you. Don't let this happen to your organization.

chapter SIXTEEN

Conclusion: How Do You Know Whether You Are Doing a Good Job?

Nonprofit marketing is, without question, a growing field. But it's still very much a young field too, especially if you take some of the concepts I've presented in this book to heart, such as becoming your own media mogul and thinking of yourself as a community organizer. There is no single job description for a nonprofit marketer. I'm not even sure we'd have it covered if we'd come up with ten different job descriptions.

Although there's a lot of fun to be had working in such a diverse field with so much pioneering going on right before our eyes, that also means it can be tough to gauge how well you are doing. Are you any good at this? If you really want to measure your success, you have to cobble together a performance review that matches your cobbled-together—and frequently changing—job description.

It's relatively easy to measure the effectiveness of many of the specific tactics that you will use in marketing; it's harder to measure some of the big-picture changes we are seeking when we market our good causes. You market your organization and its programs and services, but to what end?

As you sit back and look at your nonprofit marketing program as a whole and evaluate your own performance as a nonprofit marketer, consider these questions:

- *Does your marketing strategy make you stand out from the crowd?* Are you conveying what is unique and valuable about your organization and programs? Is it clear to the people who matter most to your success who you are and what you do? Is your marketing different enough from that of other organizations working in the same space?

- *Is your organization perceived as a leader or expert?* What's your status or reputation within your field? How does your marketing strategy help you position yourself or your nonprofit as a leader or expert? How trusted is your organization, and how does your marketing plan maintain and build trust with your supporters?
- *Do your current supporters remember who you are?* You might be surprised how many donors forget that they've made gifts to a nonprofit organization. After all, why would they remember, if the nonprofit doesn't work on maintaining those open lines of communication? Are you keeping those good feelings you worked to create through your initial outreach going strong? Are you communicating regularly with supporters? Are you reminding them what you do?
- *Do your current supporters think of you favorably?* Does your strategy include multiple ways to foster good feelings about your cause and your organization among your supporters? Or are your supporters feeling overlooked, forgotten, or used? Are you repeatedly thanking them for their support? Are you explaining the results you created, using their last gift of time, money, or talent? Are you sharing stories with them about why they matter so much to your success? Do you make your supporters, especially your biggest fans, feel like part of your team?
- *Are you connecting with new people?* Unless your target audience is a very well-defined and limited group of people without much turnover, your marketing programs should be bringing new people into your community of participants and supporters. This will often require trying entirely new approaches to tap into those networks where you don't have a presence now. Have you identified who your newest supporters will be? Are you listening to them and learning what's important to them?
- Perhaps most important, *do you love your job?*

Think about each of these questions. If you can answer a resounding "Yes!" then give yourself a pat on the back and share the secrets of your success with other colleagues. If you answer "No" or you simply aren't sure, sketch out a plan to get closer to "Yes!" in the coming weeks, months, and years.

Your nonprofit marketing work is about making the world a better place. It's important. It matters. You can do it. Thank you for taking it on.

NOTES

Chapter One: Ten New Realities for Nonprofits

1. "The Making of 'Do More Than Cross Your Fingers,'" Kivi Leroux Miller, Kivi's Nonprofit Communications Blog, September 2, 2009. See http://www.nonprofitmarketingguide.com/blog/2009/09/02/the-making-of-do-more-than-cross-your-fingers/.

Part Two: Writing a Quick-and-Dirty Marketing Plan for a Specific Program

1. Based in part on "The Great Schlep: Who Says Alienating Whole Segments of the Giving Public Is Always a Bad Thing?" by Sarah Durham, *Fundraising Success*, March 1, 2009. See http://www.fundraisingsuccessmag.com/article/the-great-schlep-403794_1.html.

Chapter Four: Define Your Audiences: Who Do You Want to Reach?

1. The Atlanta chitterlings case study comes from "The Basics of Social Marketing," Turning Point & the Social Marketing National Excellence Collaborative. See http://www.turningpointprogram.org/Pages/pdfs/social_market/smc_basics.pdf.

Chapter Five: Create a Powerful Message: What Do You Want to Say?

1. "Save the Darfur Puppy," Nicholas Kristof, *New York Times*, May 10, 2007. See http://select.nytimes.com/2007/05/10/opinion/10kristof.html.
2. "'If I Look at the Mass I Will Never Act': Psychic Numbing and Genocide," Paul Slovic, Decision Research and University of Oregon, in *Judgment and*

Decision Making, April 2007, *2*(2), 79–95. See http://journal.sjdm.org/7303a/jdm7303a.htm.

3. For more on the power of the heart over the head, see the following:

   "When It's Head Versus Heart, The Heart Wins," *Newsweek*, February 11, 2008.

   "Emotional Ads Work Best," http://www.neurosciencemarketing.com/blog/articles/emotional-ads-work-best.htm.

   "Nonprofit Marketing: The Power of Personalization,"http://www.neurosciencemarketing.com/blog/articles/nonprofit-marketing-personal.htm.

4. "Anatomy of a Direct Mail Makeover at UC Berkeley," Kivi Leroux Miller. See http://www.nonprofitmarketingguide.com/resources/fundraising/anatomy-of-a-direct-mail-makeover-at-uc-berkeley.

5. For additional information on using reason and statistics in marketing, see the following:

   "The Storytelling Power of Numbers," http://www.frameworksinstitute.org/ezine25.html.

   "Making Numbers Count," http://www.sightline.org/research/sust_toolkit/communications-strategy/flashcard5-landing-NUMBERS.

6. "Success Stories: Florida 'Truth' Campaign," Social Marketing Institute. See http://www.social-marketing.org/success/cs-floridatruth.html.

7. "The Real Darfur Puppy," Nicholas Kristof, *New York Times*, May 10, 2007. See http://kristof.blogs.nytimes.com/2007/05/10/the-real-darfur-puppy/.

Chapter Eight: Make It Easy to Find You and to Connect with Your Cause

1. "What Is WOM Marketing?" Word of Mouth Marketing Association. See http://womma.org/wom101/.

2. Excerpted from "Four Steps to Creating a Strong Nonprofit Brand," Nancy Schwartz, Nancy Schwartz & Company. See http://nancyschwartz.com/strong_nonprofit_brand.html.

Chapter Ten: Stay in Touch with Your Community of Supporters

1. "What's the Payoff? How Charities Can Figure Out How Much Time and Money to Invest in Social Networking," transcript of online chat with Beth Kanter, *Chronicle of Philanthropy*, July 21, 2009. See http://philanthropy.com/live/2009/07/payoff/index.shtml.

Chapter Eleven: Adopt an Attitude of Gratitude

1. "The No-Receipt Scandal," Jeff Brooks, Donors Power Blog. See http://www.donorpowerblog.com/donor_power_blog/2009/03/the-noreceipt-scandal.html.

Chapter Twelve: Empower Your Fans to Build More Support for You

1. "Participation Inequality: Encouraging More Users to Contribute," Jakob Nielsen's Alertbox, October 9, 2006. See http://www.useit.com/alertbox/participation_inequality.html.
2. All of the statistics on email open rates and click-through rates in this section can be found in the "2009 eNonprofit Benchmarks Study" by M+R Strategic Services and the Nonprofit Technology Network. See http://nten.org/uploads/BenchmarksPresentation_2009.pdf.
3. "Nonprofit Marketing Tip: Be Nice. It Pays Off," Kivi's Nonprofit Communications Blog, May 14, 2008. See http://www.nonprofitmarketingguide.com/blog/2008/05/14/nonprofit-marketing-tip-be-nice-it-pays-off/.

Chapter Thirteen: Find the Time: Get More Done in Fewer Hours

1. "Break Through by Taking Breaks," Matthew E. May, American Express OPEN Forum, September 17, 2009. See http://www.openforum.com/idea-hub/topics/the-world/article/break-through-by-taking-breaks-matthew-e-may.

GLOSSARY OF ONLINE MARKETING TERMS

.com, .net, .org The extension of a website address or domain name. Also called the top level domain (TLD). Originally .com was reserved for commercial sites, .net for Internet service providers, and .org for nonprofit organizations. Now anyone can purchase and use any of these TLDs. I recommend that you purchase all three for your websites.

ALT text for photos "Alternate text" used to summarize what's in an image when the image can't be viewed on a website or in an email. Assists the visually impaired who use screen readers and is also seen when images are blocked in an email.

analytics Statistics generated about visitors to a website or readers of an email. Analytics can help track which pages visitors look at, what links they click on, and how they found the site.

anchor text The text on a website or in an email that, when clicked, takes you to another place on that page or on the Internet. Anchor text is usually underlined. Also called *link text* or *hypertext link.*

blog A "web log" or online journal that is frequently updated, with the most recent updates appearing at the top of the page, in reverse chronological order.

blogosphere The collective community created by all of the blogs on a topic; the portion of the World Wide Web made up of blogs.

bouncing emails An email that is not received and is returned to the sender. A hard bounce occurs when a message is returned because the address was invalid. A soft bounce occurs when an email is returned due to a full inbox or other technical problems, even though the email address is valid.

CAN-SPAM The Controlling the Assault of Non-Solicited Pornography And Marketing Act of 2003, which established rules regarding the sending of bulk email, such as requiring an "unsubscribe" option and outlawing misleading subjects and deceptive return addresses.

click-through rate The percentage of email recipients who click on a link in a particular email message.

domain name The primary part of your website address; for examples, the domain name of http://www.nonprofitmarketingguide.com is nonprofitmarketingguide.com.

domain registrar A company that manages the registration of Internet domain names. Your domain registrar and web host may or may not be the same company.

downloads A file, such as a PDF, video, or audio file, that a user can transfer from a website to a personal computer. Some downloads are free; others you must pay for before being given access to the file.

Flash Software by Adobe (originally a Macromedia product) that allows users to create interactive animation on websites.

Google AdSense Advertising program by Google that allows website owners to place ads created by others through the Google AdWords program onto their own sites. The website owners are paid a commission by Google when someone either clicks on or views the ad.

Google AdWords Advertising program by Google that allows users to purchase ads that are placed on Google's search engine results pages as well as on Google's advertising network, including AdSense participants.

Google Alerts A free program that will alert you when keywords you select appear on the web.

Google Analytics A free program by Google for tracking website statistics.

Google Grant Program by Google that allows nonprofits to participate in Google AdWords for free. The nonprofit can place advertising on search engine results pages and throughout Google's advertising network.

Google Insights An advanced version of Google Trends.

Google Reader Google's free RSS reader. Used for subscribing to RSS feeds from blogs, news sites, podcasts, and the like.

Google Trends A tool for comparing search volume patterns for specific keywords across particular regions, categories, and time frames. The advanced version, Google Insights, provides additional analysis.

HMTL Hyper Text Markup Language. It is made up of various codes enclosed by angle brackets < >. Web browsers (like Internet Explorer or Firefox) read HTML and then display it as web pages. The same code is used to create HTML emails (emails with colors, fonts, images, and so on).

keywords The specific terms (single words and phrases) used by someone searching for something on the Internet. By knowing the keywords that best describe your organization and its work, you can track mentions of those keywords on the Internet. You can also use those words on your own website, so that search engines will associate your website with those topics.

link farm A web page that consists solely of links to other sites. Intended to help boost a website's search engine results, it is more often considered a form of Internet spam and should be avoided.

long-tail, long-tail keywords Typically, phrases with three or more words that are much more specific versions of your keywords. For example, if one of your keywords is "homeless shelter," examples of long-tail keywords are "homeless shelter for families" and "homeless shelter New York City."

microsites Mini-websites, with their own domain names, that are often created for specific campaigns. They can be independent websites or part of a larger site.

MIME Multipurpose Internet Mail Extensions, a format for sending emails that includes both an HTML and a plain text version.

open rate The percentage of email recipients who open the email message. Can be measured only for HTML emails.

opt-out Request by a recipient of an email newsletter to be removed from your email list. The recipient opts out by unsubscribing.

permalink A direct link to a specific blog post or forum entry.

permission-based email marketing Practice in which emails are sent only to those who have requested information or given permission to receive emails from a particular organization.

redirect Action taken when a user types in one website address and is automatically taken to another website address. For example, you can redirect someone who types "yoursite.com" to "yoursite.org" if you own both domain names and your main site has the .org extension.

retweet Forwarding someone else's tweet (an update on Twitter) to your own Twitter followers.

RSS Real Simple Syndication, a way for websites that are updated frequently, such as blogs or news sites, to send new content automatically to subscribers. Readers of these types of sites subscribe and then receive updates to an RSS reader, instead of having to check all the different sites all the time.

RSS reader A software tool used to collect, manage, and read content delivered via RSS feeds. For example, you can use an RSS reader to subscribe to blogs and to read the new content published on those blogs, without having to revisit the blog's homepage.

search engine Online tool used to locate information on the Internet. Google, Yahoo! and Bing are search engines.

search engine optimization Action taken to improve the effectiveness of your website so that search engines rank it higher on their search engine results pages when people search on your keywords.

search engine rankings The order in which results of a web search are listed. The most relevant websites should appear toward the top of the list. Sites are ranked according to a complex formula that includes how keywords are used on the site and how many other related websites link to the site.

social bookmarking Sharing a list of websites that you save and categorize (tag) with others. Popular social bookmarking sites include Delicious, Digg, and StumbleUpon.

social media Online sites and tools that allow people to easily create, share, and discuss content, including articles, images, and video. Includes blogs, image- and video-sharing sites, and social networking sites. Popular social media sites include YouTube and Flickr.

social media marketing Using social media sites to market a product, service, or organization.

social networking Connecting with people through an online community. Popular social networking sites include Facebook, MySpace, and Twitter.

stock photography Photos that can be purchased or licensed as opposed to hiring a photographer to produce new ones.

tags Descriptive keywords used to categorize an article, such as a blog entry or a web page a user wishes to save and share through a social bookmarking site. Tagging can help the entry be found more easily by search engines.

tweet An update sent out on Twitter.com.

unsubscribe The act of removing oneself from an email list. Can usually be done by following the "unsubscribe" link in legitimate email, but users should be cautious about using any link in an uninvited email.

URL Uniform Resource Locator, a web page's address. http://www.nonprofitmarketingguide.com is a URL.

Web 2.0 The second generation of the World Wide Web, which includes many more tools for online conversation and collaboration (social media).

web hosting Storage of your website pages on a computer server owned by the hosting company. The web host then makes the pages available to Internet users. Your web host and your domain registrar may or may not be the same company.

ACCESSING THE COMPANION WEBSITE

You'll find many additional tips, resources, and recommendations, as well as updates to material in this book that has changed since it was printed, on the companion website.

To access the companion website, go to www.NonprofitMarketingGuide.com/book and enter *bookbuyer* as the password.

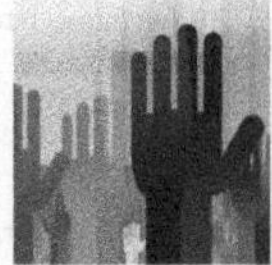

INDEX

Page references followed by *t* indicate a table.

C

D

E

F

G

H

I

N

T

U

V

W

Y

Z